OUR GOD IS
STILL TOO SMALL

By the same author

Young People Today (CYFA, 1972)
Discipleship (SU, 1978. Revised as
Discipleship: Following Jesus Today (SU, 1988)
Paul Brand (Leprosy Expert) (SCM, 1980)
God Speaks: The Bible (Lion, 1986)
The Case Against Christ (Hodder, 1986)

The Rev John Young has spent several years as a Chaplain/
Senior Lecturer in higher education. He has recently been
appointed Diocesan Evangelist in the Diocese of York.

OUR GOD IS STILL TOO SMALL

John Young

HODDER AND STOUGHTON
LONDON SYDNEY AUCKLAND TORONTO

Illustrated by John Collins

British Library Cataloguing in Publication Data

Young, John, *1937, Feb. 20–*
  Our God is still too small.
  1. Christian doctrine., God. Nature
  I. Title
  231

  ISBN 0-340-48897-2

To my Mother and to my Father-in-law,
and to the memory of their Partners

MY WARMEST THANKS . . .

. . . to the members of St Paul's Church, York – and especially to my colleague Derek Wooldridge – for their support and Christian fellowship, and for giving me time in which to write.

. . . to John Collins for his witty illustrations.

. . . to Canon John Cockerton, Jim Glaister, Liz and Mick Fryer, Marion Hoyland, Edna Mallett, Roy Stevens and Christine Woodcock for reading the typescript and/or proofs, and for making suggestions.

. . . to Juliet Newport the Editor, for her encouragement, help and enthusiasm.

. . . to Clive Calver, Margaret Cundiff, Donald English and Joyce Huggett for writing positive things about this book, and allowing them to be published.

. . . to Margaret Drake-Jones, Dimelo Middleton, Jackie Silins, Joyce Smith and Barbara Thompson for their secretarial help and unfailing kindness. My special thanks to Margaret for her initiative and hard work in researching information, and for performing miracles on the word-processor.

NOTE ON CONFIDENTIALITY

For some people, belief in God is a purely theoretical matter: an interesting topic for discussion but of little practical use. Christianity – together with other world religions – opposes this viewpoint. Faith in God and the events in our lives (often trivial; sometimes tragic) must connect. For this reason, this book contains a large number of illustrations drawn from my own life, and from the experiences of people whom I have met. In most cases there is no problem about confidentiality or recognition – but to avoid possible embarrassment, I have sometimes changed certain features (names etc), while keeping the core of the experiences which I describe.

Unless indicated, Bible quotations are from the New International Version.

FOREWORD

If you are looking for easy answers, a formula for belief which will keep you in comfort without being too demanding and which will allow you to wallow in sentimental 'hand me downs', then this book is not for you. It could disturb you, give you sleepless nights, and even push you into actually doing something about your faith.

If however you are prepared to ask yourself hard questions, and if you are prepared to accept that the answers may demand of you a radical rethink of your life style as well as your life thoughts, then this is for you!

As I have read this book I have realised how much I need to have my eyes opened to the glorious mystery of the living God. John Young addresses himself to what he calls 'the second great religious question' – *What is God like?* He provides plenty of material for us to chew on, Biblical references, quotations from a wide variety of theologians, preachers and teachers, and stories from his own experiences in his varied ministry. He does not let us evade the questions. Skilfully, thoroughly, but lovingly he takes us through the maze of complications, hacking through the undergrowth of misconceptions, brushing aside the cobwebs of outgrown theories, cleaning the lens of our dusty intellectual spectacles, so that we can begin to have a vision of the one who is the glorious mystery, yet the living, knowable God; so that, as he puts it, we have 'a loving relationship with the living God, through the Risen Christ, in the power of the Holy Spirit.'

John Young does not offer easy answers. He makes us stir ourselves, for as we follow the pointers we begin to realise that the answers are not to make us comfortable or spiritually satisfied with our arrival points, but to challenge us to action now, and 'go in peace to love and serve the Lord.' 'Amen to that,' I say!

The Revd Margaret Cundiff
Selby, North Yorkshire

OUR GOD IS STILL TOO SMALL

'As soon as I started *Our God is Still Too Small* I couldn't put it down. I think it's a splendid book. It's racily written, readable, and entertaining, yet profound, thought-provoking and at times extremely powerful; a delightful blend of wit and wisdom.' **Joyce Huggett**, author of *Listening to God* and *Listening to Others*

'John Young writes from a background of experience, not only of God's Word, but also of God's World. The challenge to a bigger view of God is significant in our generation: for too long he has been relegated to a convenient doctrine or superficial swear word. John pleads that we recover a right view; all power to his elbow!' **Clive Calver**, General Director, Evangelical Alliance

'John Young has great skill in perceiving the deep issues which face people who try to take Christianity seriously. His work amongst students has fitted him particularly for this area of perception, but he also has the gift of addressing such problems in a lively, sometimes amusing, always interesting way. And he pulls no punches. What he writes is readable. As well as helping those who actually wrestle with the problems, he will provide inspiration and guidance to those who help other people wrestle in this way.' **Donald English**, General Secretary, Home Mission Division of the Methodist Church

'He has cracked the art of being simple without talking down and he is catholic in the best sense, using examples from the breadth of Christianity.' *Church of England Newspaper*

CONTENTS

Part 1

THE LOVE OF GOD

The Christian affirmation is not simply that love *ought* to be the last word about life, but that, despite all appearances, it *is* . . . and that . . . is frankly incredible *unless* the love revealed in Jesus is indeed the nature of ultimate reality, unless he is a window through the surface of things into *God*.

John Robinson

The fully forgiven man does not rejoice in his own forgiveness but in the divine love to which he owes it; and his past sin persists in his experience no longer as a source of shame, but as the occasion of a new wonder in his adoration of the love divine.

William Temple

. . . I pray that you, being rooted and established in love, may have power, together with all the saints, to grasp how wide and long and high and deep is the love of Christ, and to know this love that surpasses knowledge . . .

St Paul (Eph. 3:17–18)

1

IS THERE ANYONE THERE?

Well, *is* there? *Does* God exist? In our century, this is the central religious question for many people. The question is put in many forms and in various tones of voice. Sometimes belligerent: go on, *prove* it. Sometimes wistful: if only . . . Sometimes hopeful: perhaps, after all . . . Sometimes desperate: please God, please be there; and please *do* something.

Very often the question is asked for a seriously practical purpose. The speaker glimpses that the question is more than a fascinating subject for debate. He or she knows that a very great deal hangs upon the answer. Is there additional strength to be had when I am at the end of my tether? Can we make sense of apparently senseless suffering? Having made a mess of my life, can I make a new start? Is there a right way through the moral maze? Do I strut around on this small planet for seventy years or so, only to be snuffed out like a candle?

If God exists, then some of these questions, and perhaps all of them, have hopeful answers. If he doesn't – if life simply began by purposeless, random chance – then not only are we without God, we are without hope, too. Macbeth is right after all: 'Life's . . . a tale told by an idiot, full of sound and fury, signifying nothing.'

Significantly, our modern question – does God exist? – is not asked much in the Bible. So it isn't answered either. Rather, the answer is assumed. Yes, he does. And that's that.

There are a few exceptions – like Ecclesiastes, that powerful Old Testament book which contemplates the emptiness of life without God. That Bible passage (and a few others, too), encourages us to ask that fundamental question about the existence or non-existence of God, and I

have attempted to sketch an answer in an earlier book. In that book[1] I survey and summarise some of the evidence for the existence of an active and loving God. And I try not to duck the difficulties which stand in the way of this belief – in particular, the great problems raised by the fact of suffering.

In this book I want to consider the second great religious question. Not: does God exist? But: what is God like? The Bible may have little to say about the first question – mainly because most people in the ancient world assumed the reality of God (or gods). In contrast, our Scriptures – both Old and New Testaments – have a lot to say about the second question. Indeed, the entire Bible can be seen as a great debate about the nature of God. A debate entitled: *what is God like?*

On page after page we see rival views of God portrayed. The prophets, poets, apostles, lawyers, theologians and historians whose words are recorded for us within the Bible, all argue for a particular view of God. And they seek to steer people away from rival views, which they believe to be false. They do so with considerable vigour and passion, because they realise that theology is essentially a *practical* business. For the way in which I understand God profoundly affects the way in which I make sense of, and live, my life.

---

[1] *The Case Against Christ*, Hodder Christian Paperback (1986).

Three examples. First, let's consider the claim of Peter Sutcliffe, the 'Yorkshire Ripper'. For several years until January 1981 he terrorised families in the north of England with appalling acts of violence. In court he stated his belief that he was responding to a divine command. He was doing God's work, he claimed, because he was killing prostitutes.

We must weigh his statement with extreme caution. He did not confine his savagery to prostitutes, and it is quite likely that he invented this story to get an 'insane, therefore diminished responsibility' verdict. But if his claim is true – if he really *did* 'hear' a voice urging him on – what are we to make of this?

Well, it is clear that the voice which he heard was not that of the Christian God. For Jesus reveals to us the God who has a particular concern and love for people on the fringe of society: people like prostitutes. That voice was nothing more than the product of Peter Sutcliffe's distorted imagination. The 'god' to whom he referred has no real existence – no existence at all outside his tortured mind. But what terrible power that imagined god unleashed!

We turn next to the Bible – to the God of the Exodus. After their miraculous escape from Egypt, where they had been abused and exploited as slaves, the Israelites found themselves wandering in the wilderness. They quickly decided that this new life was hazardous and unpleasant. In that situation we might have doubted our first impressions: perhaps the escape was not God's doing after all? But that was not their way of looking at things. They did not doubt the existence of God; instead, they wondered whether they were worshipping the *right* God.

Did Yahweh (the Lord) *really* have the power to deliver the goods? Perhaps he was a specialist God – good at planning escapes, but not so good at sustaining life? So, with Moses safely up the mountain seeking guidance, they made and worshipped another god. A golden calf. A god whom they could control. Of course, there was a lot to be said for a god who made no demands. But sadly, he could not *do* anything for them either. Their new god was too small, and their false beliefs distorted their view of reality and the way they lived their day-to-day lives.

It was the same when they settled in Canaan, the 'promised land'. Their temptation was not to give up believing in God but to hedge their bets. Starvation was a constant threat. Above all else, they needed a good harvest. Their God was good at rescue missions, but perhaps he was less good at producing milk and corn and honey. So the safe way forward was to worship the Lord, and to worship the fertility gods as well.

The prophets saw right through this. To trust in Yahweh *and* the Baals showed a lamentable lack of understanding. For Yahweh is the only God; the Creator God; the Lord of heaven and earth. Yet the other gods did have a kind of existence. They existed inside the minds and imaginations of the Canaanites – and of many Israelites, too. Dwelling there, they did terrible damage. For fertility gods make fearsome demands. In return for sending rain and sun and a good harvest, they sometimes require human sacrifice and ritual prostitution – further proof that beliefs and actions are tied closely together.

Today's world. So it is in the modern world. Most Western people believe in God. A recent survey (published in a popular British Sunday newspaper) found that about 80 per cent of people in Britain believe in God – and the figure may be higher in America. Those who would have us believe that religious belief is dying in the Western world are guilty of wishful thinking or inaccurate observation. For the findings of popular public-opinion polls are supported by careful academic research (by Professor David Martin of the London School of Economics, for example).

Belief in God is widespread. But probe further and ask the second great question, and the position becomes more complex. Ask: *what kind of God?* and you get a whole range of answers. And each of these has enormous practical implications for the way in which we live our daily lives; for the way we view the world; and for our peace of mind – or lack of it.

In this book we shall examine some commonly-held beliefs about God. Several years ago J. B. Phillips conducted a similar exercise, and he entitled his book, *Your*

God is Too Small (Epworth, 1952). My own researches suggest that we haven't made much progress. Hence the title of this book. For our God is *still* too small.

DEFENSIVE POSTSCRIPT

A story is told – in various forms by believers from different backgrounds – concerning three church leaders. I shall relate the Church of England version . . .

On his world travels, the Pope visited Dr Billy Graham, the American evangelist, and expressed interest in a bright red telephone labelled 'hot-line'. Billy explained that this phone put him directly in touch with the Almighty, and he invited the Pope to use it. Naturally, His Holiness was delighted to do so, and after the call he insisted on settling the bill. 'Very well,' said the American, 'if you insist. I'm afraid the technology required to make such a long-distance call is very expensive. That will be £300.'

The following year the Pope visited the Archbishop of Canterbury and the scenario was repeated: red telephone; conversation with God; and then the insistence that the call be paid for. 'Very well,' said the Archbishop, 'if you insist. That will be 30p.' The Pope expressed surprise at this very low cost, and explained that in America he had paid £300. 'Yes, of course,' said the Archbishop in a matter-of-fact voice, 'but from Lambeth Palace it is a local call.'

I introduce this postscript with that story, because I imagine that some readers might have raised eyebrows – even raised blood pressure – towards the end of this first chapter. For any writer who suggests that 'our God is still too small' might be claiming that he has a direct hot-line to God; or at least a clearer view of God than most ordinary mortals.

I am not. I do not claim any extra insights, nor do I believe that God has shown himself to me in a 'special' way. But I do have *some* qualifications for the rather awesome task of writing about God. Two in particular: a little leisure and a listening ear.

During my leisure I have studied the Bible and read fairly widely. Some of this reading has been in deep books about religion, but I have included 'popular' items, too. I am married with two daughters, so I am fairly up to date with teenage, women's and family magazines. These magazines sometimes carry articles which throw considerable light on widespread popular beliefs.

My reading has not been confined to religion. Novels often deal with religious topics, and as a lecturer in education I have read a fair amount of psychology. This is highly relevant, for I take seriously the link between our relationships and upbringing on the one hand, and the way in which we picture God on the other. For example, harsh parents can lead to harsh ideas about God. This reading has led me to check my own mental pictures of God against the teaching of the Bible and the views of wiser believers. As a result, I have been surprised at how wide of the mark I sometimes am in the way I picture and approach God (not that my parents were overharsh, I hasten to add!).

Reading is not my only source of information. I have learned a great deal from conversation, too. My work brings me into daily contact with people of all ages and widely-differing beliefs. Many people – believers and unbelievers alike – enjoy discussing religion, and a tame parson around the place is fair game! So while not claiming special knowledge about God, I do claim to have a pretty accurate knowledge of the fundamental beliefs held by many ordinary people. And I am troubled by much of what I read and hear – for I suspect that many false gods haunt many imaginations.

In this book I shan't be attempting to tell anyone what to believe. But I hope that every reader will be willing to re-examine his or her own beliefs about God. I say this with some passion and urgency, for I am convinced that it is an immensely important – and intensely practical – matter. For these beliefs relate very directly to a whole series of vitally important questions. Questions like: how can I find peace of mind and fulfilment in this life, and fullness of life in the next world, too?

NOTE ON RELIGION IN THE MODERN WORLD

In May 1983, the Russian novelist Alexander Solzhenitsyn reflected upon our troubled and divided world. He concluded: 'Men have forgotten God; that's why all this has happened.'[2] Solzhenitsyn spent years as a persecuted Christian in an officially atheist society, so we can feel the force of his assertion. But for some people, the reasons underlying their problems might seem quite different. Speak to a member of the persecuted Bahā'i minority in Iran, or to someone from a black shanty town in South Africa, and you might hear a different viewpoint. They might complain that men have remembered God all too well – the wrong kind of God.

What about the Western world? Public-opinion polls declare that 80 per cent of us believe in God. Does this mean that Solzhenitsyn's statement is wrong for us, too? I think not. When stopped in the high street by a woman with a clipboard, 80 per cent of us might admit to belief in God. But this does not mean that 80 per cent of us take God's law and promises into account in our daily lives. The bishop who recently described Britain as 'Godless' is not altogether wrong. For most *practical* purposes, most people live as though God does *not* exist.

Yet even that statement oversimplifies, and those who study these matters are right to remind us that the actual situation is complex. (A point which is illustrated by the fact that in some polls, more people appear to believe in prayer than in God!) I suggest that four features mark most Western countries today.

We live in a *plural* age, in which a wide range of beliefs and viewpoints rub shoulders. At the same time we are a *secular* society. Religion is often marginalised, and 'the good life' is usually based on financial security and material possessions. Yet it remains true that in some senses we belong to a *religious* society. I am not simply referring to

---

[2] In his acceptance speech for the Templeton Prize for Progress in Religion. He was quoting (with approval) a saying which he heard as a child.

prayers in Parliament, and religion in schools,[3] but to the careful research undertaken by the Religious Experience Research Unit in Oxford. This reveals that many people have experiences which they can only describe in religious terms. Far more people believe in God than attend church – and their faith is sometimes very important to them.

I recall being interrogated by a London taxi-driver. 'Up for the demo?' he asked, glancing at my scruffy coat. When I admitted that I was unaware of the demo, he tried another tack. 'Here for the conference of architects?' I felt that we shouldn't keep the guessing game going any longer, so I admitted to being a clergyman. That did it. He gave me – in colourful language – his views on the Church. Let us say that it was not his favourite organisation. Just before we pulled into Euston Station, his tone changed. 'Mind you,' he said, 'don't get me wrong. I pray. Every night, I say my prayers.' I doubt that he had admitted this to anyone for a long time, but it did not really surprise me. A hard-swearing taxi-driver, who despises the Church but believes in God and prayer, is not altogether out of place in the West today.

Above all, we are a *superstitious* society. Yesterday I received a letter from British Telecom. Printed on the envelope was the number to ring 'For Your Daily Horoscope'. Again my mind goes to a London railway terminus: Victoria this time. I arrived to find a large stall with flashing lights, and as a keen student of human nature I went to investigate. 'Your Horoscope by Computer.' This perhaps sums up modern Europe and America. We are not hard-headed atheists. We believe in fate, in luck, in the stars. Yet we like to link this with technological advance. 'Horoscopes by Computer' is the perfect combination.

The same approach can be found at a more sophisticated level. In one of her novels, the Booker Prize-winning author, Anita Brookner, writes about a refined, intelligent, well-educated woman. (Her critics say that all her novels are about such people – because she herself is all of these

---

[3] In some other Western countries the details are different, but the underlying situation is not dissimilar. For example, religion is not taught in American State schools, but 'God Bless America' is sung.

things!) Faced with difficult decisions, the central character consults a fortune-teller – and this doesn't feel out of place to the reader. It reminded me of a conversation I had with a very intelligent woman, who told me without embarrassment that she had been to see 'my fortune-teller'. She spoke in a matter-of-fact way – just as I would speak of 'my doctor' or 'my dentist'.

At the end of this brief survey I want to express my unease about this stress on horoscopes. I wonder how many people make bad decisions on the basis of what they read? But their popularity suggests that human beings are fundamentally religious. We intuitively feel that we are not 'on our own' – that there is Someone or Something 'out there'. If this instinct does not manifest itself in religion, it is likely to do so in superstition. Some critics would say that there is no difference between the two – and, of course, religion and superstition can easily slide into each other. But I strongly believe that the Christian faith points *away* from superstition; that it has a sound basis in healthy experience and in reason. The rest of this book is based on that belief.

2

GOD WHO IS BAD AT ARITHMETIC

It was Sunday morning, and I was holding a chalice as I watched people come forward to receive Holy Communion. I have done this a thousand times, and it always gives me a feeling of inner warmth – mainly because of a deep sense of kinship. For these are my brothers and sisters within the Christian family.

This Sunday was different. I felt the same warmth, but it was mixed with a measure of confusion – for this particular service was held in the chapel of a maximum-security prison. Most of the men to whom I administered the communion cup had committed terrible, violent deeds.

Were these also my Christian brothers? I knew that the answer was yes, but still the confusion remained. What about their victims? How would *they* feel about my easy acceptance of these men as brothers within a common faith? And would they be happy with the many statements in the service which express a strong desire for inner peace? Their victims might feel that God's peace is the very last thing which those prisoners deserve. Rather, they should be suffering nightmares (as some of them do, no doubt) as they relive their crimes, for they have destroyed the peace of others.

My confusion was not complete. I was not being soft and sentimental, for I was in no doubt that these men should be locked up in prison. There is no other way that society can respond to such terrible crimes. But could I view them as criminals *and* as fellow Christians? And how did *God* view the situation?

These questions drove me to take a fresh look at the second most famous story ever told. (You might pause here, and consider which titles you would select as 'the

world's two most famous stories').[1] In this story – the parable which we call the Prodigal Son (Luke 15:11–32) – we find two contrasting views of God. One of these is the Score-card God. He is alive and unwell in the minds of many people today: especially highly moral people. This God is good at arithmetic. He allocates a score-card to each human being, and on this card he awards positive marks for good deeds, and negative marks for bad deeds. At the end of our lives the points are added up, and if the ticks exceed the crosses, then we are safe.

It is easy to caricature such a view, and Tony Hancock did this brilliantly in one of his sketches. He contributed to a good cause, and declared that when he died he would wave his record of charitable giving at the Great Architect in the sky. The GA would be suitably impressed, of course.

Divine unfairness. Such caricatures are useful, but slightly misleading. They are useful for they expose the absurdity of such shallow beliefs. They are misleading because it is possible to hold this belief in a serious form – indeed the

---

[1] I judge (perhaps wrongly) the parable of the Good Samaritan to be slightly more famous than the Prodigal Son.

Bible gives some substance to this view, and we shall examine it in later chapters. However, the main emphasis of the New Testament leads us *away* from such views of God – for two main reasons.

First, this view of God can lead to despair. This was the position of the prodigal son. On his score-card he had nothing but black marks. If the situation depended on his own moral and spiritual efforts, he had very little hope. Of course, it is the elder son in the parable who illustrates belief in the Score-card God most clearly – and we can have some sympathy with his jealousy. After all, why *should* his younger brother get away with it? But the score-card idea lurked in his younger brother's mind, too. He pinned his slender hopes on his father's willingness to take him back as a hired servant. Perhaps by painful, honest toil over many years, he might repay his debts.

His father would have none of it. Instead: instant forgiveness; reinstatement as a son not a servant; the warmest of welcomes, and great joy. This, insisted Jesus, is exactly the way in which God responds to every sinner who comes to him in humble faith and sincere repentance. A clean sheet is issued. A new start is given. It may appear to be unjust – especially to those who have fewer black marks – but that is the teaching of Jesus.

God's generosity *does* seem unfair – annoyingly unfair or gloriously unfair, depending on where you stand. (Or perhaps it depends on whether you are standing at all, or lying in the dust.) This 'unfairness' is clear from the parable of the Prodigal Son; it is even clearer from the parable of the Workers in the Vineyard. Those who came to work at the last moment earned the same as those who toiled all day (Matt. 20:1–16). But total generosity is like that, and Jesus wants to lead us away from God as arithmetician, to God as generous lover.

Recently I found myself in a small predicament which illustrates the tension between generosity and strict fairness. One of my nieces is a student nurse – and very hard up. I wanted to give her some money, but to do so might have caused offence. For she has an older sister, and I didn't give money to her when she was studying. As I didn't have enough cash to make a useful gift to both, I had two possible courses of action. I could withhold the gift (my niece did not know of my intention, so this would be easy and safe), or I could take the risk.

The parallel is limited, for the problem presented by God's generosity is that he treats us *all* – apparently good and obviously bad – with undeserved love. But it does illustrate the tension. Strict fairness can stand in the way of open-handed generosity.

Now let's return to that prison chapel. Without a generous Gospel, which declares the mercy, grace and forgiveness of God, those men would have no hope whatsoever. If the Score-card God is enthroned in heaven, those prisoners could do nothing but despair. Because of their crimes they would have no chance of scoring enough good marks to outweigh the bad – for even a million acts of kindness cannot atone for loss of limbs and life. But the Bible is clear in its teaching: *everyone without exception* is included in God's offer of free, complete forgiveness. Which is just as well. For if God were to act strictly according to the score-card, *none* of us would be safe – not even the highly moral elder son in the parable. Which brings us to my second main point.

As we have seen, belief in the Score-card God sometimes leads to despair. Just as often it leads to pride.

The prodigal son had one quality in large measure: humility. He was not self-deceived. He knew that he deserved no favours whatsoever, for his predicament was entirely his own fault. If standards of strict fairness were applied to his situation, he was lost. Even the slender hope that his father would accept him as a hired servant depended upon his father's mercy. Strict justice would require: 'Get out and don't come back!' In contrast, the elder son concentrated on his own achievements. His younger brother's antics made this easy, for compared with him he was virtue itself.

In the pages of the Gospels we meet many people who think as he does. They inhabit a world of rules, regulations and strict arithmetical fairness. Do this; don't do that. By virtue of their upbringing, their circumstances and a strongly-disciplined personality, they are able to keep the

rules. All around them they see other people struggling –
and failing. So they feel superior and secure. It is summed
up brilliantly in one little story told by Jesus, which takes us
to the heart of the Gospel (Luke 18:9–14; *see* Postscript).

Keeping the rules is not unimportant. Jesus made this
clear. But humility is a vital ingredient, too. For if keeping
the rules leads us on to spiritual pride, we are in deadly
danger.

Certain kinds of pride are innocent enough. I am proud
of my children's achievements; you are proud of your
garden. There is nothing wrong with that: it amounts to
simple satisfaction in honest effort. But to be proud of
myself and of my own moral and spiritual achievements:
that is another matter altogether. And if my ability to keep
the rules leads me to compare myself with those who don't,
then my pride highlights two dangerous blind spots.

First, spiritual pride makes it impossible for me to enter
into another person's situation. *Why* is he like that? Why
does she behave in that way? Given the upbringing which
they had, might I not be the same – or even worse? 'There
but for the grace of God go I . . .' isn't always a cliché.
Second, this kind of pride also shows that I am unaware of
the real quality of my own inner life. If I concentrate on my
positive deeds, all might seem well. But if I consider my
inner motives, my thought-processes and all the acts of love
which I could have done but failed to do, I might see the
score-sheet very differently.

Respectability. This has been illustrated in our century by
two men of intellectual brilliance. C. E. M. Joad was a
philosopher and broadcaster, who became a convinced
Christian towards the end of his life. In part, this was
because he came to recognise the poverty and inadequacy
of his own inner life. Measured by ordinary standards of
morality he was fine – Cyril Joad was no football hooligan!
But measured by the standards of love, and against the
teaching and example of Jesus, he came to see himself as a
sinner who was greatly in need of grace and forgiveness. In
Recovery of Belief (Faber, 1952) he wrote:

Up to that time I had been, I think, agreeably immune

from the sense of sin . . . and I am not proposing to indulge in the luxury of personal confession. Let it, then, suffice to say that my eyes were gradually opened to the extent of my own sinfulness in thought, word and deed; so . . . it was only with great difficulty and effort that I could constrain myself to even the most modest degree of virtue, and that very rarely . . .

Professor C. S. Lewis is widely known for his many books – especially his children's stories based in Narnia (*The Lion, the Witch and the Wardrobe* is the most famous). He became a believer at an earlier point in his life than C. E. M. Joad. In his spiritual autobiography (*Surprised by Joy*: a Fount paperback) he explains how gradually – and reluctantly – he edged his way towards faith in the Christian God. One important moment came when he caught a clear insight into his own motives and thought-processes: 'For the first time I examined myself with a seriously practical purpose. And there I found what appalled me; a zoo of lusts, a bedlam of ambitions, a nursery of fears, a harem of fondled hatreds. My name was legion.'

Now both these men were highly respectable. They were not Jekyll and Hyde. But an attempt at honest – not morbid – self-examination, led them to see that something was seriously wrong: *so* seriously wrong that they were less in need of direction and correction than of mercy, grace, forgiveness and a completely new start. In other words, they needed the *unfairness* of God. They needed a God who would not treat them strictly according to their just deserts. They needed a God who would tear up the score-sheet, and give them a fresh start and a new life. It is just such a God that Jesus proclaimed as his Father – and ours.

Those two highly intelligent men saw that their situation was similar in kind (while being very different in degree) from those worshippers in the prison chapel. So they heard the words of Jesus gladly: 'It is not the healthy who need a doctor, but the sick. I have not come to call the righteous, but sinners' (Mark 2:17).

POSTSCRIPT

1 *Encouragement from Archbishop Desmond Tutu*

What a tremendous relief . . . to discover that we don't
need to prove ourselves to God. That is what Jesus came
to say, and for that he got killed . . . The Good News is
that God loves me long before I could have done anything to deserve it. He is like the father of the prodigal
son, waiting anxiously for the return of his wayward son
. . . That is tremendous stuff – that is the Good News.
Whilst we were yet sinners, says St Paul, Christ died
for us. God did not wait until we were die-able, for He
could have waited until the cows came home (*Hope and
Suffering*, Collins, 1983).

2 *Our tasteless God*.

In a play by Alan Bennett, a dis-
illusioned Vicar's wife laments, 'But that's the thing no-
body ever says about God . . . he has no taste at all.' How
true – for he loves you and me! But this is not the *trouble
with* God – it is the *graciousness of* God. Jesus highlights
this in his parable about the Pharisee and the tax-collector
(well worth reading: Luke 18:9–14). He ends that story by
stating that the sinful but humble tax-collector 'went home
justified before God.'

Professor Joachim Jeremias drew attention to that little
word 'justified'. He believed that St Paul's central doctrine
of 'justification by faith' was based on this parable. Certainly the mood of that doctrine is anticipated by Jesus
here. It points to a sentence in St Paul: 'For it is by grace
you have been saved, through faith – and this not from
yourselves, it is the gift of God – not by works, so that
no-one can boast' (Eph. 2:8–9).

3

'Lord Jesus Christ, Son of God, have mercy on me a
sinner.' The ancient 'Jesus Prayer' used widely in the
Eastern Orthodox Church.

3

GOD WITHOUT GARBAGE

We sat and drank coffee. He was in a bad way: depressed, upset and unkempt. In an outburst of frustration he had thrown one of his few possessions – a bicycle – down some steps and smashed it. Now he was in the middle of a crisis of confidence, and he needed help. Above all, he needed friendship and reassurance. His life, he felt, amounted to nothing. He had achieved nothing; he was less than nothing. That was his own assessment. Was he correct?

Through my work I come into contact with a wide range of people, with a wide variety of problems. From time to time I meet individuals who are deep in depression, and I am well aware that it takes more than a few well-chosen Bible verses to meet their needs. But on this occasion I felt that a particular Bible passage might be worth considering together. For he was a fellow-believer, and a major aspect of his problem was a deep-seated sense of worthlessness.

He knew lots of 'successful' Christians – people who follow Jesus with a real measure of determination and joy. Their success, and the importance which some of them place on 'victorious Christian living', only emphasised his own sense of inadequacy. He could believe that God loved *them*, but as for him . . .

So I took my Bible from the shelf and read two verses, 'A bruised reed he will not break, and a smouldering wick he will not snuff out, till he leads justice to victory. In his name the nations will put their hope' (Matt. 12:20–1). St Matthew makes it clear that these aren't his own words. He took them from one of the 'Servant Songs' which feature in the book of the prophet Isaiah, and applied them to Jesus. *Why?*

Encouragement. The evangelist did this because he wanted

to emphasise the *gentleness* of Christ. Matthew is not afraid to show the fierceness of Jesus. When confronted with hypocrisy, or with those who laid heavy burdens on other people (especially religious burdens), Jesus was very fierce indeed (Matt. 23). But with the down-trodden and heart-broken he was very, very gentle.

'A bruised reed he will not break'. In the Palestine of Jesus, as in modern Israel, reeds came in various strengths and sizes. The largest – called *arundo donax* – grows as high as 3 metres. These reeds were used for a variety of purposes. Short lengths would serve as pens. Medium lengths were used as flutes (I have one, bought from a street trader in Jerusalem). Longer sections were used as fishing spears, measuring-rods or walking-sticks. At his crucifixion, Jesus was offered a sponge containing vinegar. It was held up to him *on a reed*.

For all these purposes, strong undamaged lengths were required. A bruised reed would be floppy and useless. You could not write with a bruised reed pen, play a tune on a damaged flute, or catch fish with a bent spear. So you would throw it away, cut yourself another length and start again. This was an everyday occurrence, which Isaiah's hearers and Matthew's readers would readily understand.

So we can see why Matthew quoted this passage from Isaiah. He wanted his readers to compare God with the Israelite who used a reed for one of these practical purposes. Or rather to compare *Jesus* with that Israelite. Which amounts to much the same thing. For both Isaiah and Matthew refer this passage to God's special representative – to God's servant (Isaiah); to God's Son (Matthew). And the wonderful truth is that God's representative does not behave like everyone else. For unlike other people, he does not discard bruised reeds. *He has no rubbish heap*. He finds *some* use for them all.

The same point is made in the second illustration from this short passage. 'A smouldering wick he will not snuff out'. Oil-lamps were common, and essential, household objects. The people of Jesus' day were adept at trimming a wick to the correct length. If a lamp gave off smoke instead of light, it was useless. So the householder would snuff out the wick, trim it off, discard the remnant and start again.

Here is a second wonderful contrast. Jesus does precisely the opposite. He perseveres. He does not trim the wick. Gently he blows, until the smouldering glimmer gives off light. Or if the trouble is lack of fuel, he pours more oil into the lamp. He does not give up, and he has no discarded trimmings.

Of course, Isaiah and Matthew weren't particularly interested in reeds and wicks. They were greatly interested in *people*. And so was Jesus. Especially humble, hurt people. This passage amounts to a wonderful promise. We may sometimes feel worthless and useless. But we are wrong. For Jesus will persevere with us. He treats us with love, gentleness and patience. 'A bruised reed he will not break, and a smouldering wick he will not snuff out.'

Fifty not out. This wonderful truth is spelt out in other places in the Bible, too. Recently I had a crisis of confidence myself, triggered by one of those significant birthdays with an '0' at the end. It is not unknown for a fortieth birthday to precipitate a 'mid-life crisis', but crisis-points can be reached much earlier. I know of a girl who wept on reaching 20, in the belief that her best years had gone! In my case it was the flood of '50 not out'[1] cards which prompted me to do a little personal stocktaking.

What did my twenty years in the ministry of the Church add up to? Nothing much really. When I did the natural – and foolish – thing of comparing myself with other obviously 'successful' Christian ministers, I felt even worse. Then I 'discovered' a verse in one of St Paul's letters. It comes at the very end of that great chapter which he devotes to resurrection (1 Cor. 15). In that passage, Paul stretches language to its limits. It is a glorious affirmation of all that the resurrection of Jesus means – nothing less than the defeat of death itself.

When he reaches that great climax, the reader is aware that Paul ought to stop, for it is impossible for him to add anything important on this great theme. But he doesn't stop. So the end of the chapter is marked by a definite

---

[1] Those coming to terms with middle age might enjoy *Half Way* by Bishop Jim Thompson (Collins, 1986).

anticlimax. For he brings us back from heaven, and right down to earth – back to our daily work. 'Therefore, my dear brothers, stand firm. Let nothing move you. Always give yourselves fully to the work of the Lord, because you know that your labour in the Lord is not in vain' (1 Cor. 15:58).

This verse was a tremendous encouragement to me in my disappointment and depression. Resurrection is about our future hope; *but it is a present reality, too*. Because he rose from the dead, Jesus is alive for evermore. And because he is alive, he walks with us day by day. So – because of his resurrection – our lives and our daily work are never useless. Our 'labour in the Lord is not in vain.' Just as Jesus worked a wonderful miracle when the small boy gave him five loaves and two fishes, so he works a wonderful miracle with the daily offering of our lives and our work. It may not amount to much in our eyes. But he accepts our small offerings, then he blesses and multiplies them. For this reason, our 'labour in the Lord' is never fruitless.

Then I noticed something else. St Paul was not writing to Christian ministers. He was writing to lay people, many of whom were Corinthian slaves doing very ordinary household chores. It was to them that he first gave this promise. In other words, it does not apply only to our 'Christian activities' or to church work. It applies to *all* our activities, however ordinary, which are done in his name. He accepts such offerings, and he lovingly sweeps them up into his great ongoing purposes of love for the world.

God keeps no rubbish bin. He discards no one. He refuses nothing that is offered. Instead, he has a special affection for ordinary people – especially those who are humble and hurt. Jesus put it this way: 'But many who are first will be last, and many who are last will be first' (Matt. 19:30).

Jesus said, 'Come to me, all you who are weary and burdened, and I will give you rest. Take my yoke upon you and learn from me, for I am gentle and humble in heart, and you will find rest for your souls. For my yoke is easy and my burden is light' (Matt. 11:28–30).

Teach me, my God and King,
In all things thee to see;
And what I do in anything
To do it as for thee . . .

A servant with this clause
Makes drudgery divine;
Who sweeps a room, as for thy laws,
Makes that and the action fine.

George Herbert

POSTSCRIPT

1 *On loneliness*. At the end of Chapter 1 we noted four
key features of modern life. At this point I want to add one
further point. It arises from the sense of isolation and
worthlessness which characterised my friend, whom I described at the beginning of this chapter. For it is clear that
we live in a *fragmented* society. I recall listening to the
author of a book on the Arctic. He told us about an Eskimo
who was asked to give his opinion of the Americans he had
met. The Eskimo paused. Then he said, 'You are very
clever . . . and you are very lonely.'

This was reinforced for me when I dialled a wrong
number. It was a rainy Sunday lunch-time, and I needed
train information for a visiting preacher. The phone was
answered with great speed and enthusiasm, and I could
hear the acute disappointment at the other end when I
made my request. 'Oh,' she said, 'You've got a wrong
number. I am so disappointed. I've been on my own for
hours, and I thought someone was calling for a chat.'

It was one of those occasions when we have bright ideas
far too late. I couldn't think of an appropriate response, so I
apologised and put the phone down. Then I thought of all
the things I might have said – but I had no idea which
combination of figures I had pressed.

That woman illustrates the fragmentation of much modern life – especially in large cities, where people in bed-sits
often don't know the people on the next floor. Fragmentation can lead to freedom, of course: our behaviour is not
scrutinised as it would be in a small, settled community. But

fragmentation can also lead to isolation and alienation.
Modern society badly needs places with open doors and
welcoming friends. Clubs, pubs and adult education classes
have a part to play. So, I hope, do churches.

2   *Encouragement from Cardinal Newman.*

God has created me to do him some definite service, he
has committed some work to me which he has not
committed to another. I have my mission – I may never
know it in this life, but I shall be told it in the next.

I am a link in the chain, a bond of connection between
persons. He has not created me for naught. I shall do
good, I shall do his work. I shall be an angel of peace, a
preacher of truth in my own place *while not intending it* –
if I do but keep his commandments.

Therefore I will trust him, whatever, wherever I am, I
can never be thrown away. If I am in sickness, my
sickness may serve him, in perplexity, my perplexity may
serve him, if I am in sorrow, my sorrow may serve him.
He does nothing in vain. He knows what it is about. He
may take away my friends. He may throw me among
strangers. He may make me feel desolate, make my
spirits sink, hide my future from me – still he knows what
he is about.

4

FOOLISH GOD

People sometimes say, 'One day I will write a book.' Those who do, find that their task is a mixture of enjoyment (those days when the pen flows over the page) and hard work (getting up at 5.30 a.m. so that you don't lose the ideas which come to you in the night!) The stage in writing a book which I dislike most is that point when final decisions have to be made. Should I ditch that? Do I keep this? Shall I alter that? In order to help with these decisions I ask a few people to read the manuscript and make comments. Sometimes I get two or three clued-up Christians to check the accuracy and the theology, and two or three people with little church involvement to check whether the words on the page make sense to the proverbial woman in the street.

At this stage in my previous book, one copy of the manuscript came back with a comment which sticks in my mind. I had quoted the words of Jean Vanier who founded L'Arche (The Ark), a network of small communities providing love and care for handicapped people. He wrote, 'We all have to choose between two ways of being crazy; the foolishness of the Gospel and the nonsense of the values of the world.'

Against this sentence one of my readers had placed a question-mark. She asked: 'I thought you were a Christian. What on earth do you mean by calling the Gospel, "foolish"?' Fair comment! But that risky description was not mine – nor Jean Vanier's. It comes in the Bible, where we find phrases like 'the foolishness of what was preached' and 'the foolishness of God' (1 Cor. 1:21, 25). What *do* we mean by talking about a 'foolish God' – which would be regarded as blasphemy in some religions? At least three things:

1   The God Who Runs

I am grateful to Colin Chapman[1] for drawing my attention
to a tiny but highly significant phrase in the parable of the
Prodigal Son. Just two words, but they say a great deal:
'. . . he ran'. I have read that verse (Luke 15:20) scores of
times without seeing its significance; now it 'hits' me every
time. *Recap*. The younger son left home with a substantial
share of the family fortune and squandered it on reckless
living. After falling on hard times he plucked up courage to
return home, in the hope that his father would allow him to
work as a hired servant. His father refused. Instead he went
two extra miles. He saw his son in the distance and . . . 'he
ran'.

Now middle-aged, property-owning fathers in the
Middle East do not run. For appearances are important,
and running is undignified. Besides, men in positions of
leadership should keep their feelings under control, except on appropriate occasions like funerals and weddings.
Running is for children, not for sober adults. But on this
occasion the father was so overjoyed that he forgot about
his dignity. He picked up his skirts *and he ran*. What is
more, he ran a considerable distance. For he spotted his
son 'while he was still a long way off'.

The children had a wonderful time. First they were able
to gather round the ragged tramp who stumbled into their
village. How different he had looked on that day when he
strode out with such arrogance! You can almost hear the
giggling and see the pointing fingers. The village children
soon forgot about the son, however, for they were dis-
tracted by an even more remarkable sight. They gawped in
amazement at this usually dignified man, holding up his
skirts and running down the street. In no time they had
transferred their mirth and laughter from the younger, to
the older, man.

It is clear that welcoming his son in this way carried a high
personal cost for the father. Had he waited on the doorstep
with coolness and decorum until the son had come *to him*,
he would have survived the incident with his dignity intact.

---

[1] Colin Chapman based his comments on books by Kenneth Bailey and on conversa-
tions with a friend who lives in the Middle East.

No doubt the trouble continued when the elder son heard that his father had made a fool of himself. Whispered taunts probably continued for months afterwards. 'He's gone soft. He should have treated his son as he deserved . . .'

So the parable of the Prodigal Son could be renamed the parable of the Foolish Father. Which is good news for us. For the son in the parable represents you and me in our rebellion, our waywardness and with our need for forgiveness and restoration. The father in the parable represents God: our foolish God.

This points us forward to the foolishness of the Gospel. It is foolish because, before it displays God in his power (by the resurrection of Jesus), it depicts God in his self-inflicted weakness. Jesus – the Lamb of God – bears the sins of the world on Calvary, and God refuses to intervene. It is certainly not a question of God the Father venting his anger upon his Son. *Both* consented to this terrible deed. *Both* suffered. For 'God was in Christ reconciling the world to himself' (2 Cor. 5:19 RSV).

It is because of their great concern for the dignity of God and of his prophet (as they describe Jesus), that Muslims refuse to accept that Jesus died on the cross between two thieves. For they see very clearly that if he *did* die there, then Calvary is not a place for sentimentality, but a place of rejection, of shame, of humiliation and degradation. In some art, Christ appears to be *pretending* on the cross. 'Don't worry,' he appears to say, as he looks down benignly. 'I'm all right really. For I am the Son of God, so it isn't *really* hurting.'

But Jesus did not simply appear to be suffering; he *was* suffering. As Lord MacLeod of Iona put it: 'Jesus was not crucified in a cathedral between two candles, but on a cross between two thieves; on the town garbage heap; at a crossroad so cosmopolitan that they had to write his title in Hebrew and in Latin and in Greek . . . at the kind of place where cynics talk smut, and thieves curse and soldiers gamble.'[2]

---

[2] George MacLeod ends his purple passage on a severely practical note: 'Because that is where he died. And that is what he died about. And that is where Churchmen ought to be, and what Churchmen should be about.'

We can be grateful for the deep concern to uphold the honour of Jesus shown by our Muslim friends – but we must dissent from their conclusions. For Christians see the cross and resurrection as the pivotal events in all history. Jesus rose *from the dead*. Which means that he did not merely *pretend* to die. It is by these means that a fallen world is to be redeemed; it is by these methods – and no other – that a divided and troubled world will be reconciled to God, and with itself.

It was human pride which opposed Jesus; it was human ignorance which mocked Jesus; it was human greed which betrayed Jesus; it was human sin which crucified Jesus; and it was human death which enveloped Jesus. God took these evil things and used them as the raw materials from which to quarry our salvation. Truly, the foolishness of God is wiser than the wisdom of men!

2 The God Who Stands

The humility of Jesus is seen at its starkest on the cross. But it is reinforced at every point in his life. The King of Kings is born, not in a fine palace, but in a simple stable. He grows up to develop the hard hands of a carpenter. At his baptism he does not stand with the one who baptises, but with the ordinary people who come to be baptised. He never fully reveals his glory to the world which he came to save; always there is the possibility of misunderstanding and rejection.

This is demonstrated very clearly in the temptation narratives. Jesus went into the wilderness to sort out his strategy. It would be highly convenient to use methods which the world understands so well – a display of un-mistakable power would do the trick in no time. Instead, he chose to walk the way of the cross. If people are to decide for him, it must be for the right reasons. He will offer them wonderful things – homes, brothers, sisters, mothers, chil-dren, fields and eternal life (Mark 10:30). But that particu-lar package-deal ends with a single tell-tale word: his offer involves 'persecutions', too.

His humility continues to this day. Many old Prayer Books contained a print of Holman Hunt's famous picture entitled *The Light of the World*. It is based on a famous verse in the final book of the Bible. 'Here I am! I stand at the door and knock. If anyone hears my voice and opens the door, I will come in and eat with him, and he with me' (Rev. 3:20). In that verse and in that painting, we see the risen, ascended and glorified Christ. St John, who painted this verbal picture, earlier saw the splendour of the risen Lord in a vision on the Isle of Patmos. So overwhelming was the sight that 'he fell at his feet as though dead' (Rev. 1:17). Yet this same risen Lord comes to each of us in great humility. He will not force an entry into our lives. Instead, he stands patiently on the threshold and seeks a personal invitation to come in. He could take us by storm, but that is not his way.

So it is with his work in the world. Having provided a wonderful Gospel, he is extremely careless in his after-sales service. 'The Word became flesh and made his dwelling among us . . . full of grace and truth' (John 1:14). 'Christ Jesus came into the world to save sinners' (1 Tim. 1:15). Such a glorious message demands a score of heavenly messengers. Nothing less than a whole fleet of angels and archangels will do! But no. Instead, God entrusts this treasure to 'earthen vessels' or 'clay pots' (2 Cor. 4:7). In other words, God entrusts his message to . . . *us*. To ordinary, fallible, squabbling human beings; and to that very imperfect organisation known as the Church. It is rather like visiting an exhibition of the Crown Jewels, and finding them displayed in a series of cardboard boxes.

In the winter of 1987/8 some of the terracotta soldiers who guarded the tomb of the Chinese Emperor Qin Shi-huang (who lived about 200 years BC) were exhibited in London. I heard the organiser speak about the headaches presented by safe transportation. Every possible precaution was taken. He had sleepless nights, and the insurance costs were astronomical.

This is an exact reversal of the way in which God treats the treasure of his Gospel. He makes a priceless gift – nothing less than a fine pearl of great value (Matt. 13:46). But in transit it is hardly protected at all. It bumps around in the Church, in the lives of ordinary Christians and in the world. It is handled by all comers. What foolishness! What confidence! For who needs expensive insurance when God himself is overseeing the enterprise? For while he genuinely does entrust the Gospel to us, he does not withdraw his interest and activity. The New Testament speaks of the apostles not only as workers *for* God, but as fellow-workers *with* God.

3 The God Who Speaks

As I write this paragraph, there are two books on my desk. One is a car manual. It has a clear index, designed (not always successfully!) to enable the reader to find clear answers to all his questions. The other book is a Bible, which is sometimes described as the 'Maker's Manual'. This can be a useful description, for the Bible provides guidance for living, deep insights into what has gone wrong, and directions for those who want to get back on course. But we must not press the comparison too far. For the Bible tells a story. It is much less 'tidy' than a handbook, a thesis or a manual. So we cannot always turn to this page or that for clear answers to all our questions. These sixty-six books (which took over a thousand years to complete) have coherence and unity, because they tell the history of a people.

They claim to describe for us the relationship and interaction between God and the human race. The *way* in which they do this is highly significant and points once again to the foolishness of God. For by communicating with us in this way, God ensures that there is ample opportunity for misunderstanding. How well Jews and Christians have exploited those opportunities. How foolish of God, who should have known better!

Some faiths have a much more logical approach to their Scriptures than Christianity. It makes good sense to regard a special book – and Scriptures are that by definition – as being special in *every* way. So the Church of Jesus Christ of the Latter Day Saints, claims that the Book of Mormon was written on special tablets in a special language. Muslims assert that the prophet Muhammad received the Koran by direct dictation from the Archangel Gabriel. Such books are therefore exempt from the questing minds of men. There is only one fitting response: submit![3]

In contrast, the process by which we have received the Christian Scriptures is much less tidy. Instead of doing the job properly, by doing it *himself*, God chose to include us – not as passive recipients, but as active agents. '. . . men spoke from God as they were carried along by the Holy Spirit' (2 Pet. 1:21). Christians refer to the Bible as the Word of God. But it is also the work of men – and their limitations show through. Ungrammatical Greek, outbursts of rage and a limited understanding of God's love[4], mingle with glorious literature, wonderful passages on the supremacy of love and forgiveness and deep insights into eternity. Yet God takes every page and speaks to us through it.

Even primitive views about God point forward to the One who will fulfil and transcend all the earlier promises. For we are wrong if we read the Bible as a 'flat' text. It is dynamic and on-the-move. For example, Leviticus provides insights into an understanding of God which were vitally important, but which have been transcended, left behind and fulfilled. This does not mean that we can throw Leviticus away. Reading that book helps us to understand the holiness of God, and the way in which God prepared the world for the sacrifice of Jesus. But it is of little *direct* relevance to us now, for animal sacrifice belongs to the past – to the days of preparation.

Or consider the cowardice of Peter in betraying Jesus; or the end of Psalm 137, where the Psalmist displays bitterness against his captors:

---

[3] Islam literally means 'resignation' – to the will of God.
[4] For example, see Psalm 137: 8–9 on page 32. Or we might consider Exodus 15:3 where we read that 'The Lord is a warrior'. This concept of the Lord leading his troops in battle is retained and 'spiritualised' in the New Testament. Jesus waged war against the powers of darkness. His disciples are called 'soldiers' because he requires them to fight against evil in his name – opposing injustice in the world at large, and fighting sin and selfishness within their own lives. But literal 'holy wars' fought with guns and bombs are far removed from the spirit of the New Testament.

> happy is he who repays you
> for what you have done to us –
> he who seizes your infants
> and dashes them against the rocks
>   (vv. 8–9).

These things are not included in the Bible as examples to be copied; but they are included for our consideration. I believe that God intends even that dreadful passage to be included, for he wants us to see the *poet* as well as the *poem*. The Bible is about real people, not cardboard cut-outs. He wants us to see the way in which they thought and reacted. But when we are tempted to cowardice (like Peter), or revenge (like the Psalmist), we shall be wise to ponder the teaching of Jesus alongside these other passages.

At the centre of the story is the God of the Covenant – the One who gives, and renews and refines his glorious promises. The One who keeps his word. He takes the long view. Not yet . . . not yet . . . not yet. Yes, it *will* happen, but in *my* time and in *my* way – not in your time and in your way. Then at last it *did* happen. Two Bible verses sum up the result: 'This is my Son, whom I love. Listen to him!' (Mark 9:7). 'For the foolishness of God is wiser than man's wisdom, and the weakness of God is stronger than man's strength' (1 Cor. 1:25).

POSTSCRIPT ON THE BIBLE IN TODAY'S WORLD

1   *A book for all ages*. I was told about a man from China who started to read the Bible. After a while he said: 'Whoever made this book, made me: it knows all that is in my heart.'

I know exactly what he means. Last year I heard a radio programme on the Crusades, and I could not identify at any point with those men of a thousand years ago. Their attitudes and outlook were utterly different from mine. I was reminded of the words with which L. P. Hartley opens his novel, *The Go-Between*: 'The past is a foreign country; they do things differently there.'[5] But press back a further thousand years into the world of the New Testament, and I hold a mirror to myself and to my world.

Of course the culture was different. Of course I have to struggle at several points to get 'inside' the outlook of the New Testament writers. But those writers deal with the 'constants' in human life: with the things that do not change. They deal with love and hate; with forgiveness and mercy; with the way I spend my money and use my time; with my attitudes to the poor; with life and death. They deal with these issues profoundly, and in a way which speaks to every generation.

Some passages deal with issues long since dead. For example, in his first letter to the Corinthians, St Paul raises a tricky question. Should Christians who go out to lunch with their non-Christian friends, eat meat which has been 'offered' to idols? No doubt some Christians somewhere in today's world, face this problem. But for most of us it is totally irrelevant. Dead as a dodo. Yet . . . while the problem of meat offered to idols isn't our problem, the *principles* raised by it are vital for modern life. For example, we should seek the good of others; we shouldn't deliberately shock or offend other people; love is crucial – even more important than knowledge (1 Cor. 8:1–13).

It is also true that answers to many problems in the modern world can't be 'read off' from the pages of the Bible. I am thinking of questions concerning the alleged nuclear deterrent, and ethical issues of life and death raised by medical science. But we find basic guidelines in the Scriptures – and we look to the Spirit of the living God to help us apply this teaching to today's problems.

2   *A transforming book*. A 16-year-old murdered a member of a rival gang in Singapore, for which he was sentenced to life imprisonment. The prisoner in the next cell passed to him ten pages from the Gospel of St Luke, so he read and

---

[5] Some periods of history are more congenial than the Crusades, of course; and I joyfully agree that the Bible is not the only old book which contains insight and inspiration.

reread the words of Jesus. Slowly he understood, and asked for God's forgiveness. To his surprise, he was released from prison. Now he is helping ex-prisoners and drug addicts to put their shattered lives back together.

3 *A sustaining book*. Sir Geoffrey Jackson was British Ambassador in Uruguay. In January 1971 he was captured by terrorists. For several months he experienced terrible conditions: he was kept in a tiny cell, and he knew that at any moment he might be killed. His diplomatic training and his Christian faith were a tremendous help in his 'people's prison'. Eventually he was given books, and a bed. Two books were particularly important to him. One was Leo Tolstoy's great novel, *Anna Karenina*. The other was a Bible – first in Spanish, then in English.

4 *The greatest book*. Brian Redhead, one of Britain's most popular broadcasters, recently read the Bible from cover to cover. Then he presented a series of radio programmes, and wrote a book entitled *The Good Book* (BBC, 1986). On being interviewed by Norman Ivison about the project he replied:

> It's really a journey through life. It makes sense of the universe we find ourselves in. The story line is tremendous. I think people forget what a good tale it tells – the story of the Children of Israel is the greatest story ever written anyway; and then [with] the coming of Jesus you have a whole new song being sung. So once you get into it, you find that it holds together . . . But also it's so diverse . . . It's like having a great compendium of friends. It just is *the* greatest document of the lot, and once you've read it, your life is never the same.

5 *A book to be read*. 'Normally we read as quickly as possible, because we are reading newspapers, light fiction, etc. Or when we are studying a subject, we read as critically as possible. For a change, try reading suitable parts of the Bible as lovingly as possible – lingering over the scene, noticing every detail as if you had been there, asking what it shows you of God. Such "meditation" on the Bible supplies

a solid basis for prayer – and life. When you have got clearer in your mind the reality of God, coming to you in Jesus, stepping out of the pages of the Bible, you will find it easier to put together the jigsaw puzzle of your life.' David L. Edwards, Provost of Southwark Cathedral.

POSTSCRIPT ON THE LOVE OF GOD

In his foolishness, God does not give us water-tight proofs for his existence, nor for his love. It is my conviction that there is ample evidence for both, and that this evidence finds its focus in Jesus. But we live by faith not by sight, nor by proof – and sometimes God's love breaks into our lives despite our unbelief.

For example, in *Contemplation in a World of Action* (Unwin, 1971), Thomas Merton writes about a young married woman who was an atheist. She was interested in Christianity but found the evidence unconvincing. One day a priest refused to argue with her and simply told her that God loved her and wanted her heart. Thomas Merton comments, 'All of a sudden this whole thing collapsed and there broke through into her heart the sense of who God really is and what He really meant to her. She saw how desperately she needed this God who loved her, who was calling her to accept His love and to love Him in return. The whole reality of the thing just simply burst through.' He adds, '. . . let us pray for an increase of faith and give ourselves totally, completely, and with perfect confidence to the God who loves us and calls us to His love.'

5

LUCKY CHARM GOD

A couple of years ago I interviewed four students – two men and two women – for a series of television epilogues. Not one of the students was much over 20, but each of them had lived interesting and tough lives. One interview in particular stays in my memory.

When she was 10, Judi's brother had been killed in a road accident. Four years later, her father committed suicide. Young as she was, those terrible events forced her to look hard at her fundamental beliefs. Her conclusion was surprising. Those two deaths did not lead to a loss of faith in God, but to a rejection of her previous understanding of what that belief implies.

Until her father's death, Judi's God was like a mental lucky charm. Most of the time she lived without giving much thought to him. But when a problem arose (like illness), or when a hurdle stood in her path (like an exam or a difficult decision), Judi would take this little God from her mental pocket, dust him down and ask for his help.

Faced with real problems of a daunting size, she realised that her view of God was little different from keeping a handy idol on the mantelpiece. She came to see that her mental picture of God cut him down to a ridiculous size – not a real God, but a lucky charm. She viewed him as a genie in a Christmas pantomime. He was at her beck and call, but he remained safely inside the lamp until she rubbed it. When tragedy struck, she realised that this picture of God was extremely inadequate. Yet she was able to rescue *something* from those earlier ideas, even though her God was far too small.

At the other end of the spectrum are those who believe in God, but who think that he is unlikely to be interested in the events in *their* small lives. Sometimes this conviction

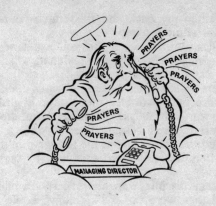

arises from a belief that God is great but distant. Sometimes it springs from an unexamined mental picture of God as a harassed businessman who cannot quite cope. He is already very busy running a universe and trying to answer 'telephone calls' from Earth (the prayers of those who desperately need his help). To pile on one more request – especially a non-urgent request – would break the camel's back (capital 'C' for this particular Camel, of course)[1]. So they take pity on this tired God, and refuse to join the 'God-botherers'.

If I had to choose between Judi's lucky charm God, or the distant God, or the picture of God as a harassed managing director, I should opt for the first every time. For he is involved in our lives and he is competent to help in some degree. But there is a better way forward than any of these – a way forward given by Jesus himself.

Jesus' teaching about God as Father
First, a simple task: can you spot the foreign words in the following sentences?
1   His speech caused a great furore.

---

[1] In fact, because God created time and lives in eternity, he has 'all the time in eternity' to concentrate on every single individual. (This idea is developed in Chapter 7.)

2 You scratch my back and I'll scratch yours; that is
   known as a quid pro quo.
3 Please lick the envelope before you post it.
4 Kai elegen, abba ho pater, panta dunata soi.

The answers to questions 1–3 are obvious enough, even
though we accept the word 'envelope' as an English, as well
as a French word nowadays. The answer to question 4 is less
obvious, unless you read Greek. Even so, some readers will
have spotted the word *abba* as the foreigner in the fourth
sentence. It is this tiny word that is significant for our
discussion.

Jesus and his disciples were almost certainly bilingual. In
this regard they were rather like many people in North
Wales today, who can change from Welsh to English in
mid-sentence. (An English friend who is married to
a Welsh girl, told me that his wife speaks with her parents
in Welsh. When he joins them, they switch instantly from
Welsh to English in order to include him. He added that he
will worry if the day comes when they change *from* English
to Welsh on his arrival!)

In Jesus' day the Greek language was widespread and the
Aramaic tongue was much more localised. So the New
Testament was written in Greek, in order to reach as many
people as possible. But because Jesus so often spoke and
taught in Aramaic, some of his original words are found in
the New Testament. Mark in particular includes Aramaic
words in his Gospel: *Ephphatha* and *Talitha koum*, for
example. These foreign words are embedded in the original
Greek of the New Testament. Clearly, they are phrases
which stuck in the minds of Jesus' hearers.

One striking example is found in Mark 14:36, where we
see Jesus in deep anguish in the Garden of Gethsemane. It
was the night before his arrest, and he prayed: 'Abba,
Father, everything is possible for you. Take this cup from
me. Yet not what I will, but what you will'. (For the Greek
form of the first half of this sentence, see question 4 above).

Research. A tremendous amount of research has been put
into that little word Abba, and two conclusions stand out.
First, the word was not used in prayer by Jewish leaders at

the time of Jesus. Second, the word was very common – not in a religious setting, but in a *domestic* setting. It was the word commonly used by young children when addressing their fathers. In the same way they would use the word Imma, when talking to their mothers. (I wrote the first draft of this chapter on a train, and when I got to this paragraph a child from the next table called across the gangway, 'Dad, can I have a drink?' This is a perfect example of the way in which young Jewish children would have used the word, Abba. Its nearest English equivalent is 'Dad' or 'Daddy'.)

It was almost certainly Jesus' custom to address God in this way, and it is a clear example of the mixture of old and new which marked his teaching. Jesus did not come up with a brand-new set of original ideas, for he was conscious of standing in a God-given tradition. Instead, he took familiar concepts. With these he made new connections and from these he drew fresh insights.

The word Abba illustrates this, for Jewish teachers *did* address God as Father. But usually their approach was slightly formal – in the same way that a Victorian son might address his influential father as 'Sir'. Jesus took this important notion of God as Father one step further, and addressed him with the intimate family word: Abba.

But that is not the end of the matter. Read on in the New Testament and you come to the letters of St Paul. In two of these – his letters to Galatia and to Rome – we also find the word Abba. For example, '. . . you received the Spirit of sonship. And by him we cry, "*Abba*, Father." The Spirit himself testifies with our spirit that we are God's children' (Rom. 8:15–16).

This is totally unexpected. We can understand a Galilean like Jesus using an Aramaic word, for it was his native tongue. But the Church in sophisticated Rome was made up of people who did not speak Aramaic at all. Yet within thirty years of the death of Jesus (and even earlier in the case of the Christians in Galatia), Paul can assume that this particular word is well known and well understood, hundreds of miles from Aramaic-speaking Palestine.

It is as remarkable as finding a single Welsh word in frequent use in the American Senate. Clearly, Abba had become a Christian catchword: it was loaded with meaning which Paul did not need to explain to a non-Aramaic speaking church. It is not surprising to find Jesus addressing God as Abba – not only because he spoke Aramaic, but because he enjoyed such a close relationship with God. It is very surprising indeed to find it used in the non-Aramaic-speaking church in Rome.

The explanation is clear enough: Jesus gave this word as a gift to his followers. And not just the word, *but the close and intimate relationship which it depicts*, as well.

Practical. This has tremendous practical implications for the way in which we approach God in prayer and trust him in our daily lives. For good parents are interested not only in the big events in their children's lives. Of course it matters to them a great deal whether their children pass their exams; whether they marry (and whom they marry!); and whether they find suitable jobs. But good parents are concerned with smaller matters, too: the games their children play, their cuts and bruises, their likes and dislikes, their tears and laughter. By encouraging us to approach God as 'Abba, Father', Jesus makes it clear that God is interested in *every* aspect of our day-to-day lives.

An enjoyable rebuke. The implications of this were spelt out for me by a mature student – a married man with two young children. He and his wife managed on very little money, and paying the bills was a struggle. One day he told me that he intended to continue studying after gaining his degree – for Kevin believed that God was calling him into the ordained ministry. This would mean two more years as a student. His wife supported him; it was a joint decision.

I was delighted, but dismayed too. For I wanted to spare that family the difficult years which lay ahead. I expressed my concern, and he looked at me with mild surprise and amusement. 'What is the point of being a Christian if you don't put your faith to work?' he asked. 'God will provide for us, as he has done in the past. If we don't take his promises seriously, then for all practical purposes we are atheists, even though we say the creed in church on Sundays.'

Seldom have I enjoyed a rebuke so much! That brief

conversation made concrete and particular for me all that is involved in calling God 'Abba, Father'. The old saying is true: if a thing is big enough to *worry* about, it is big enough to *pray* about. St Peter must often have heard Jesus use the word Abba in his prayers and in his teaching. As a result he was able to write: 'Cast all your anxiety on him because he cares for you' (1 Pet. 5:7).

Who of you by worrying can add a single hour to his life? . . . But seek first his kingdom and his righteousness, and all these things will be given to you as well. Therefore do not worry about tomorrow, for tomorrow will worry about itself. (Matt. 6:27, 33–4).

POSTSCRIPT

1 *Swimming and diving*. A comparison is sometimes made between swimming and discipleship. Paddling is fun – but tame. *Real* exhilaration is to be had in the rough and tumble of the waves. It is the same with following Christ. We find real fulfilment only when we take our feet off the bottom and take the challenge of his teaching seriously.

We might draw another comparison between *diving* and faith. I recall standing on a very high diving-board and looking gingerly over the edge. I lacked the courage to dive, but I was determined to jump. In one way, this was the simplest thing in the world. All that was required was something which I do every day – to put one foot in front of the other. But while it was straightfoward and uncomplicated, it seemed very challenging and risky indeed! Active faith is like that. It is simple and uncomplicated – but it sometimes takes everything we've got.

2 *Faith and fear*. Fear is a universal experience, and Christians are not exempt. Some fears are rational and lead to sensible behaviour – like locking doors. Some fears are irrational, and both kinds of fear are sometimes overwhelming – fear of insects; fear of the dark; fear of the unknown; fear of death . . . Simone de Beauvoir (a close friend of the atheist philosopher Jean-Paul Sartre: see page

174) wrote movingly about a sense of rising panic as her middle years ticked by. In her youth she probably felt immortal; no one had prepared her for this strong desire to stop the clock. But she couldn't . . . 40, 41, 42 . . .

Jesus was a realist. Time after time he uttered the little phrase, 'do not be afraid' – because he knew that his disciples, like everyone else, would be afraid of all manner of things. I think it was Pastor Richard Wurmbrand who (in prison) counted the number of times the phrase 'fear not' comes in the Bible. 366. One for every day of the year, including a leap year. How like our God to think of every detail! (Confession: I haven't checked Richard's arithmetic!)

'Do not be afraid, little flock, for your Father has been pleased to give you the kingdom. Sell your possessions and give to the poor' (Luke 12:32–3).

3   Cardinal Hume on faith and holiness.

Holiness involves friendship with God. God's love for us and ours for him grows like any relationship with other people. There comes a moment, which we can never quite locate or catch, when an acquaintance becomes a friend. In a sense, the change from one to the other has been taking place over a period of time, but there comes a point when we know we can trust the other, exchange confidences, keep each other's secrets. We are friends. There has to be a moment like that in our relationship with God. He ceases to be just a Sunday acquaintance and becomes a weekday friend (*To Be a Pilgrim*, Basil Hume. SPCK, 1984).

Academic footnote: I based my comments on *Abba Father* on the work of Professors Joachim Jeremias and James Dunn. Recently, Professor James Barr has criticised aspects of their approach. It is a technical argument, but the outcome of this scholarly debate does not affect the main thrust of this chapter, for James Barr is not casting doubt upon God's fatherly care nor upon the wisdom of active faith. Indeed, he concludes: 'The importance of the fatherhood of God for Jesus is amply evidenced in many places and is not in question here.'

6

ODD-JOB GOD WHO CHANGES NAPPIES

Recently I received a long, irate letter from a man who had read one of my books. He is an atheist, with an adult son whom he described as 'a maniacal Methodist'. In his letter he levelled many complaints against the Church, against my book, and against his son. He was particularly incensed by a recent incident concerning a breakdown of their family car, which refused to go at a most inconvenient moment. Alternative arrangements were made, but before going back to the stationary vehicle, his son prayed. This time the car obligingly started, and his son thanked God for answering his prayer. His father protested. How *could* an intelligent man possibly believe in an Odd-job God?

This reminded me of a heated discussion on a radio programme. A woman phoned to say that her daughter wanted a flute, but she could not afford to buy one for her. So she prayed, and soon afterwards an unexpected cheque arrived. At that time our television screens were daily showing pictures of famine in East Africa. The phone lines were hot. How dare that woman pray for a flute when millions of children were starving? And how dare God answer such a piffling prayer, while apparently ignoring really urgent matters?

We shall examine this issue in greater depth in a later chapter, but I want to start that hare running now because the previous chapter requires it. On the basis of Jesus' teaching that God is Abba, Father, I repeated the time-honoured Christian teaching – if a thing is big enough to worry about, it is big enough to pray about. Car break-downs and flutes in hard-up families cause a lot of worry. So if the old teaching is true, they ought to generate a lot of prayer as well.

You will gather from this that I am on the side of the

'maniacal Methodist' son, and of the woman who phoned in
to the radio programme. If parents in employment are
prepared to work hard in order to buy flutes for their
children, then I don't see why parents without earning-
power should not pray for the same thing. But I am also on
the side of the father and of the radio protestors. (I believe
this is known as having your cake and eating it too!)

When is a prayer not a prayer? The Christian God is not an
Odd-job God. If he were, he would be nothing more than a
Lucky Charm God in thin disguise. He is Abba, Father –
which means that he is concerned for all our concerns,
however trivial they might appear to other people. But he is
even more concerned for our *growth*. If our prayers are
selfish, we shall remain stunted. So I shall pray happily
about a car breakdown or an expensive gift for my child –
provided I am also praying for other people, whose needs
are so much greater.

I suspect that the two Christians whom I mentioned
above have wider horizons than their own immediate
needs. If they haven't, then they have learned little about
the Christian way. An unprecedented tide of money flowed
in for famine relief at the very time that they were praying
about cars and flutes. Their urgent prayers for Ethiopia
may have been part of the reason for this. For I do not
accept that God did nothing in response to the prayers
offered by multitudes of people who were deeply
concerned about that famine.

I shall end this short section with another example which has also been known to raise howls of protest. Some Christians drive into town and pray for a parking-space as they travel. Now I am in two minds about this. Parking *is* a problem, and we are encouraged to pray about things which worry us. But this can breed a selfish approach to life. I am able-bodied, and well able to walk from the multi-storey car park on the edge of town. So perhaps I should pray for elderly or handicapped drivers whose need of a parking-space is much greater than mine.

On occasions I do pray about trivial matters like this – if I am in a great rush, or if my car breaks down at a tricky time. But I do not expect God to alter the laws which govern the internal combustion engine, for I believe that he has created the universe with an inbuilt reliability. If God altered the laws of physics to get me out of a minor jam, then he would do so for other people, too. That way lies chaos. This does not mean that we should not pray about small matters, nor that miracles do not happen. Nor does it mean that God won't prompt other people to come to my aid in answer to that shortest and most urgent of all prayers, ('Help!') It *does* mean that the living God is greater – much greater – than the Odd-job God.

The Gospel of prosperity. It will be appropriate at this point to say a word about the 'prosperity gospel'. This is associated with American televangelists, but it comes in more subtle forms as well. 'Turn to God and you will prosper' is the basic message of this 'gospel'. Of course, it does work like this sometimes. When people are converted to Christ they receive a new purpose in life. Many individuals have put their lives in order and worked hard as they have followed the Christian way. Result? Material prosperity. But to suggest that it always works like this is quite false.

Yes, Jesus *does* make wonderful promises. But he makes tough demands, too. Obedience might mean taking a job with a lower wage. It will certainly involve sacrificial giving. Many Christians are *worse off* as a result of their faith – and glad to be so, for they know that 'their' money and possessions are not theirs in an absolute sense. They are for sharing. So they do not ask, 'How much of *my* money should I give to God's work?' but: 'How much of God's money – of which I am a steward – shall I spend on myself?'

Nappy-changing God

For Christmas I was given a Trivia diary. It is an ideal companion for places like a dentist's waiting-room. Facing the appointments pages are sheets of useless but interesting information. For example: do you know which song is sung more than any other in the Western world? Well, I guess that no one can really know the answer to that, but the suggestion given seems very probable. (Those with enquiring minds are referred to the end of this chapter!) This question led me to wonder which song is the biggest hit of all time. I came to the conclusion that it might well be Psalm 23: 'The Lord is my shepherd, I shall not want.'

That song has been around for nearly 3,000 years, and it continues to be sung thousands of times each week. It brings encouragement to those who are getting married; it brings comfort to those who are dying or bereaved; it sustains many in their daily routine. But I know of one man who rejected the Christian faith on the basis of that psalm. He reasoned like this . . . Sheep are mindless; they follow where they are led without thinking for themselves. They are – in both senses of the word – *woolly*.

This objection links with other Christian teaching. If Abba is the word used by young children, and if God wants us to be converted so that we become like little children (Matt. 18:3), it looks as though he wants to keep us in nappies. It is *bad* parents who so enjoy their children's dependence that they don't want them to grow up and to think for themselves. Perhaps God is like that? This criticism made me think hard, and I would offer to that man, and to others who feel the force of his objection, the following reflections.

(a)   *The way images work*. 'The Lord is my shepherd' (Ps. 23:1). '. . . we are the people of his pasture, the flock under his care' (Ps. 95:7). This is vivid picture language. The Bible is full of it, and we need to understand how it works.

Metaphors, or verbal pictures, are very like their big brothers – parables. Which means that they are usually designed to draw our attention to one central truth. In this case we are intended to focus on *the care of the shepherd*, rather than on the 'woolliness' of the sheep. This is particularly clear from the loveliest shepherd passage of all:

> He tends his flock like a shepherd:
> He gathers the lambs in his arms
> and carries them close to his heart;
> he gently leads those that have young
> (Isa. 40:11).

God's concern for the perplexed sheep is so great that he leads and directs; his love for the lonely sheep is such that he will not leave them comfortless; his compassion for the lost sheep involves him in seeking them out; his care for the wayward sheep is so profound that he, the Good Shepherd, will lay down his life for them.

(b) *Maturity matters*. From the frequent use of word-pictures in the Bible, I draw the *opposite* conclusion from the man who gave up his faith. For the possibility of misunderstanding which is built into verbal images and parables, shows that the authors want us to grow up and to think for ourselves. This is particularly true of Jesus, who made strong demands upon the thinking powers of his audience. Most of his hearers were uneducated country-folk – practical people like shepherds, fishermen, carpenters and housewives. Yet Jesus had a very high regard for their intelligence.

Sometimes his teaching is unmistakably clear. But very often he is deliberately confusing and ambiguous. He taught that God is a heavenly Father, and stressed the vital importance of love and forgiveness. So his hearers knew that he didn't mean it when he told them that God is like an unjust judge (Luke 18:6), or that they should hate their parents, spouses and children (Luke 14:26). He left them in doubt and confusion.

In this way, he stirred their minds into furious activity, and left wide open the possibility that they would draw the wrong conclusions. He was content to leave them wondering: 'What on earth does this man mean?' A risky way of teaching! But modern educational psychologists assure us that this is sound teaching method.[1] Pose puzzles and raise questions; challenge settled ideas; stir the mind into action. These are the ways which lead to growth and understanding. The mind is more like a muscle which needs exercise than a sponge which soaks up information. It is clear from the Bible that God does *not* want to keep us in nappies. Quite the reverse; he wants us to grow to maturity.

(c) *Independence is an illusion*. All this talk about needing God as Father, friend, and saviour makes some people feel that Christians are a wimpish bunch. Grow up! Stand on your own feet! Yes, but . . . Dependency is a fact of life and independence is often an illusion. I eat a modest breakfast, but before I set out for work I am dependent upon the labours of men and women in at least two continents. It is the overprotected, immature person who pretends that he is adequate on his own. (I recall a quip about a self-made man, who worshipped his maker.)

As well as being an illusion, *in*dependence is a luxury which few can afford. If I am wealthy, well-bred and healthy, I can convince myself that I pay my own way, and that I have a right to the things which I buy and use. Which is another way of saying that I have a right to expect others to labour on my behalf – whether directly (as servants) or indirectly (as makers of cars, builders of houses, and growers of food).

Think a little harder and we see that none of us did anything whatsoever to deserve or earn the basic raw materials of our lives. We had no say in whether we were born into wealth or poverty. Equally, we have no say as to whether we are good-looking or ugly, clever or dim. These things make us what we are, so we tend to think of them as 'ours' in an absolute sense. They are not. 'From everyone who has been given much, much will be demanded,' said Jesus (Luke 12:48). One day we shall be required to give an account of our stewardship.

---

[1] Especially those working in the field of cognitive development, such as the Swiss researcher, Jean Piaget.

Some modern writers (Christian and otherwise) put this point very graphically. They speak of being 'thrown' or 'dumped' into this world. We did not ask to be born; we had no say concerning our circumstances or gifts. We simply 'arrived' – helpless. As St Paul put it: 'What do you have that you did not receive?' (1 Cor. 4:7). The answer is clear. Nothing; absolutely nothing at all. The fact that we were not born into a poor Asian family, or with multiple handicaps, has nothing at all to do with us – except as recipients.

At first sight it looks as if the Ethiopian caught up in widespread famine, is more dependent upon other people than the rest of us. On reflection this is seen as a smoke-screen – and the exact opposite of the truth. For it is a fact that each person reading this book uses more of the world's energy, food and human resources, than twenty Ethiopians. The more wealthy we are, the more dependent we are – on the labours of others, and on having access to an unfair proportion of the good things in this world.

The New Testament is more interested in the notion of *inter*dependence than *in*dependence. We all have one thing in common: we are totally dependent upon God. Without his creative love and upholding power we should not exist at all. And we are all dependent upon one another. The Church is called 'the body of Christ'. Gifts are sprinkled among all its members, and God has arranged things so that no one person has them all. Those few gifts which I do have are not intended for personal indulgence. They are 'for the common good' (1 Cor. 12:7) – to be pooled and shared. In addition, we are called to 'Bear one another's burdens, and so fulfil the law of Christ' (Gal. 6:2 RSV).

(d) *Grow up*. Once we have grasped our dependence upon God and on other people as inescapable facts of life, we are set free for a *mature* form of independence. I know of intelligent people who have made tough decisions to leave comfort and security behind. They have taken great risks and accepted demanding tasks: their faith in God has not kept them in nappies. The New Testament calls us to be childlike (not childish: see page 63). It also demands maturity. The balance is beautifully struck in 1 Cor. 14:20: 'In regard to evil be infants, but in your thinking be adults'.

POSTSCRIPT

1   *Psalm 23*. Carl Burke, an American prison chaplain, encouraged the young men in his care to probe the Scriptures by making a free translation into their own idiom. One of them started Psalm 23 like this:

> The Lord is like my Probation Officer,
> He will help me,
> He tries to help me make it every day . . .
> Because I trust him, and that ain't easy,
> I don't worry too much about what's going to happen.
> Just knowing he cares about me helps me.

I suspect the original poet would be happy with that.

2   *One body*. The *inter*dependence of the different parts of the body was forcibly brought home to me when our children were young. Our daughter cried on a very cold night and I went in to comfort her. I forgot that we had put a low-wattage heater in her room, and I kicked it with the little toe on my left foot. The result could not really be described as my little toe aching. Rather, it was *me* aching – the focus just happened to be at the end of my left leg!

When day came and the pain had lessened, I reflected on the truth of St Paul's famous passage about the Church as the body of Christ: '. . . there should be no division in the body, but that its parts should have equal concern for each other. If one part suffers, every part suffers with it; if one part is honoured, every part rejoices with it' (1 Cor. 12:25–6). As I looked at my bruised toe I understood that passage more clearly than ever before!

'*Answer*' (see page 46) Happy birthday to you. (Now kick yourself because it's so obvious!)

7

BLUEPRINT GOD

Simone Weil was a brilliant Frenchwoman whose life was charted by tough, controversial decisions. She was a philosophy teacher, but she chose to identify with ordinary people by working in France's vineyards and in the Renault car factory. Despite her faith in Christ, she refused baptism and declared that the only person she envied was the bad thief who was crucified with Jesus. She dare not aim higher than that.

During the Second World War she came (reluctantly) to England to work for the French provisional government. Throughout that period she identified with her own Nazi-dominated country as completely as possible. She refused to eat more food than she would have got in occupied France. So she became ill and died (penniless) in 1943.

It is clear that Simone Weil faced a whole series of difficult decisions. Yet she confessed that she hated decision-making. At one point she admitted that her idea of heaven was to be free of all decisions. 'The most beautiful life possible has always seemed to me to be one where everything is determined, either by the pressure of circumstances or by impulses such as I have just mentioned and where there is never any room for choice' (*Waiting on God*. Collins, 1951).

Many people would echo that – and many Christians think that they have the ultimate get-out as far as decision-making is concerned. Put the responsibility on to God. For he is the good shepherd – and shepherds guide their sheep.

Finding the Plan. Some people talk in terms of God's blueprint for their lives. They believe that God has a plan for them mapped out in advance, and they ask God to make

the pattern clear. I agree that there is some value in this approach, but I have serious reservations about the way in which it is sometimes applied. For it can shift our attention from the right question (How can I *do* God's will?) into a guessing game called, 'Hunt the blueprint'.

There are some passages in the Bible which appear to encourage us to believe in the Blueprint God who has everything mapped out. Jeremiah was prepared for his work as a prophet from his mother's womb. Ephesians 2:10 declares that God has prepared 'in advance' good works for us to do. And it is clear that God knows the future as well as the past. This is a difficult concept, so we shall pause for a moment in an attempt to 'unpack' it.

When he was in dispute with the Jewish leaders, Jesus said: '. . . before Abraham was born, I am!' (John 8:58). In this way he referred back to an Old Testament passage in which God revealed himself to Moses. 'I AM WHO I AM' (Exod. 3:14). Now it is true that Old Testament scholars differ in their interpretations of the divine name. But this, and other Bible passages, suggest that God is 'the eternal present tense'. To him, everything is . . . *now*. For he created time as well as space, and he is greater than either.

We live out our lives along a time-line. In the year 2000, we shall look back to 1990, and forward – but without knowledge – to 2010. God is 'outside' time, for his 'home is in eternity' (Isa. 57:15 JB). This means that he can see 1900, 2000 and 2010 'all at once' (I use a time phrase because I am bound by time and have no alternative). If this paragraph isn't helpful, I suggest that you put it on one side, for I readily admit that it is very crude. The central point is that God knows what will happen in what is (to us, but not to him) 'the future'. But this does not mean that the future is fixed.

In the film *Lawrence of Arabia*, I recall a scene in which T. E. Lawrence is trekking across the desert when he realises that one of the camels is missing. His companions try to discourage him from going back, for he might die in the burning sun. To dissuade him they say, 'It is written' – by which they mean that Lawrence cannot alter the time 'set' for the death of the camel and its rider.

This view is widely held today in the West. It is found in a popular form among the large number of people who believe in fate, or in luck, or in the stars, or in destiny. Everything is settled. If it is our destiny to die on a certain day; if our 'number' is on the bullet, then nothing we can do will change the inevitable. 'It is written.'

Lawrence disagreed. 'It is *not* written,' he asserted as he turned his camel back for the risky journey. In other words, we are not puppets. We can take real initiatives and actually alter the course of events. The lives of the camel and its rider *could* be saved. Some Christians come dangerously close to the superstitious 'it is written in destiny' approach to life – although they dress it up in suitable spiritual language, of course! They reason like this: God has a blueprint for my life. Therefore it is vital that I get every step right – especially every big decision. Because if I don't, I shall stray outside 'the plan'.

I know of a Christian who lived in torment for several years, because he believed in the Blueprint God. He felt he had made a wrong decision and taken a wrong turning a few years earlier. As a result he was convinced that the rest of his life was doomed to be lived according to a second-rate emergency plan. I believe this to be a false and tragic view of God's interaction with us.

For one thing, there is no such thing as a doctrine of Christian infallibility. True, we have the Scriptures to direct us, God's Son to inspire us, and God's Spirit to guide us. It remains true that 'we all make many mistakes' as St

James put it (Ja. 3:2 RSV). God's relation to us is dynamic, not static.

An illustration from music helps me to grasp this. On the radio I heard a composition called Riley's 'In C'. The composer did not write set notes and he did not give hard and fast rules to be followed by the players. Instead, he gave broad principles and key ideas, and asked the players to co-operate in the composition of the music – which was different each time. In contrast, Bartok wrote his string quartets with a whole set of detailed instructions to the instrumentalists, in an attempt to get the notes, the pace and the mood, exactly as he wanted them.

In his relationship with us, God is much more like Riley than Bartok.[1] He gives us guidelines – and a lot of space. Imagine that I have made what I now regard as a bad decision. Does this mean that I have lost my way, or strayed from the plan? Perhaps. If so, does this mean that I must settle for second-best for evermore? No! He is the God of new beginnings. Today is the first day of the rest of my life – and yours, too. In our imaginations we can hear God say: 'It doesn't matter *where* you happen to be in life's maze, for I am greater than your circumstances. If you want to make the most of your life then offer it to me, and from that moment on we'll make the best of it together. Take heart, for I shall prepare endless good ways for you to walk in.'

He does not say this just once; he perseveres. God does not offer us a blueprint. Instead, he offers us *himself*. And he has no second-best. For '. . . we know that in all things God works for the good of those who love him' (Rom. 8:28).

POSTSCRIPT

1 *An encouraging carpet.* I was told of a collective which designs and weaves handmade carpets. If a member makes a mistake, they do not unpick it. They respond to this by

---

[1] For any Bartok fans who read this, I should add that he took a more flexible approach in his later sonatas.

sitting down together and discussing how the design can be altered to accommodate the new factor. Sometimes the result is *better* than the original design. An insight into the creative manner in which God works in our lives, perhaps?

2 *A famous sentence*. 'Sin is behovable [inevitable], but all shall be well and all shall be well and all manner of thing shall be well' (Mother Julian of Norwich).

3 *An example of God's guidance*. Albert Schweitzer is one of the great figures of the twentieth century. He was a leading authority on Bach, and a radical theologian with an international reputation. One day he read a magazine of the Paris Missionary Society which spoke of the need for missionaries in the Congo. The article ended like this: 'Men and women who can reply simply to the Master's call, "Lord, I am coming," those are the people whom the Church needs.' So he enrolled as a medical student, and embarked on his life's work as a doctor in Equatorial Africa. His decision was controversial, and some saw it as a waste of his unique intellectual powers. It can be understood in the light of this paragraph from his most famous work of theology:

> He comes to us as one unknown, without a name, as of old by the lakeside he came to those men who knew him not. He speaks to us the same word: 'Follow thou me,' and sets us to the tasks which he has to fulfil for our time. He commands. And to those who obey him, whether they be wise or simple, he will reveal himself in the toils, the conflicts, the sufferings which they shall pass through in his fellowship, and, as an ineffable mystery, they shall learn in their own experience who he is.

Part 2

THE LIVING GOD

I am the resurrection and the life.

(John 11:25)

Jesus is not merely alive; he is brimful of life – the source of all life.

Trevor Reed, lay preacher, in an Easter sermon.

Salvation is not a theoretical doctrine . . . (see page 68)

Christ the Sun of Righteousness shine upon you and scatter the darkness from before your path . . .

Advent Blessing

8

KILLJOY GOD

My temporary presence in the school helped to solve a small but tricky problem. It was an independent school in Scotland and I was there at the invitation of the chaplain. I arrived a few hours before the annual staff dinner, and my host had been kind enough to include me. The tricky problem was presented by the arrival that term of a female teacher, in a previously all-male school. Wives were not invited to that particular dinner, but Miss Jones was, for she was a member of staff. One woman among dozens of men. So they solved two minor problems at one stroke – by placing the new art teacher next to the visiting clergyman.

I expected a slow, easy-going start to our conversation, but I was mistaken. Before the soup arrived, she turned to me and spoke out with the vigour of someone who enjoys a good argument. 'The trouble with you Christians is that you're a bunch of necrophiliacs.' Before attempting a reply, I glanced at the menu again. Five courses. This was going to be a long, demanding evening!

Necrophiliacs. Lovers of death. That word has one very unpleasant meaning, but as we talked it became clear that she was accusing Christians of being negative and gloomy – lovers of death, not lovers of life. Her accusations arose from painful childhood experiences of close relatives who worshipped a Killjoy God. In view of this, what could I say?

Sadly, I did not say anything very profound. The meal had numerous interruptions: fresh courses, bagpipes and interesting speeches. I was grateful for every one of them! So our conversation was not as continuous nor as intense as I feared. But since that evening I have reflected on her outburst. How *can* Christians respond to the accusation that their God is a killjoy and that their faith takes the sparkle out of life?

This accusation was made at its sharpest by the Victorian poet, C. A. Swinburne, when he declared: 'Thou hast conquered, O pale Galilean; the world has grown grey from thy breath.' As Swinburne saw all around him a religion of duty which contained many negatives (Thou shalt not . . .) he felt sad; even angry. Christianity seemed to be squeezing the fun out of life. His attitude is not uncommon today. But because religion is less central in today's society, sorrow and anger have largely given way to mild contempt or indifference. In the light of the accusation that God kills joy, what can Christians say?

Defence. Well, this particular Christian would say several things. In the first place I agree that the danger exists. As a modern monk put it, 'In attempting to become unworldly, you can beome grim.' With that sentence firmly in mind I would point to the Fourth Gospel, where the evangelist reports Jesus as saying, 'I have come that they may have life, and have it to the full' (John 10:10). The stated aim of Jesus was not to diminish, but to *expand* our lives. In the jargon: Christianity is 'life-affirming'. Indeed, some would go as far as to say that the main purpose of the mission of Jesus was to make us fully human.

At this point I shall take the risk of asserting that his intention appears to have succeeded remarkably well in some lives. I am thinking of famous saints like Francis of Assisi, Dietrich Bonhoeffer and Mother Teresa. But I also have in mind people whose holiness and joy in life are unknown outside their own locality, as well as some whose damaged lives seem to be held together by fragile threads of faith.

This view is shared by others. For example, in *The Way The World Is* (SPCK, 1983) John Polkinghorne writes:

> I have to say that in my experience most of the people I know who impress me most as being open to reality, deep in perception, firm in love, are also Christian believers. Of course, not all. I gladly acknowledge these qualities in friends who stand outside the faith. But there does seem to be a special quality in people who live close to God.

Of course, there's a lot more to Christianity than one verse in St John's Gospel which stresses 'life', supported by a few examples of lives apparently enriched by faith in Christ. A large number of New Testament passages appear to *confirm* the accusation that Christians are 'lovers of death'. Certainly the crucifixion of Jesus is given great prominence, and the cross has long been *the* symbol of the Christian faith. Nevertheless, this New Testament stress on the death of Jesus is in fact a stress on *life* – and I hope an illustration might make this clear.

Life from death

In his fine book, *Miracle on the River Kwai* (Collins, 1963), Ernest Gordon describes the same basic situation which has been immortalised by the novel and film, *Bridge on the River Kwai*. His book is a personal account of true happenings within those terrible prison camps. (This is not intended as a racist or anti-Japanese remark. *All* nations commit dreadful acts in wars). One event stands out in my memory.

At the end of a hard day's forced labour, a squad of British prisoners reassembled. They and their tools were counted, and one shovel was missing. The guard insisted that a member of the working party had stolen it. He became very angry, and demanded that the guilty person should own up. No one did. The guard's anger turned to rage and he threatened to shoot every member of the patrol. It was clear that he meant what he said, and he was about to begin when one man stepped forward and said calmly, 'I did it.' In response, the furious guard clubbed him to death on the spot. Later, the tools were recounted. A mistake had been made: no shovel was missing. Ernest Gordon comments, 'As this story was told, remarkably enough, admiration for the Argyll transcended hatred for the Japanese guard. News of similar happenings began to reach our ears from other camps.'

The result of such heroic acts of self-sacrifice was highly significant. First, the men whose lives had been saved were deeply grateful. Every new day seemed like a gift. Without their friend's heroism they would be dead: his death meant life for them. Second, they were challenged and inspired. They wanted to express their gratitude for the fact that he had saved their lives. The only way to do this was by modelling their lives upon his sacrificial death.

So a new mood began to emerge. Instead of hoarding and hiding occasional 'goodies' which came their way (understandable enough when you are close to starvation), the men became more open and generous. Not only did that prisoner's death save them physically – it liberated them *mentally*, too. Their attitudes changed profoundly. They were 'converted'. When they looked back to that significant death (as they often did), they were not being morbid, for it was a vital source of renewal and life.

A parallel

There is a striking parallel here with the death of Jesus and our response to it. Christians believe that Jesus laid down 'his life for his friends' (John 15:13). They believe that his death was a saving act – rather like the death of that soldier, but operating at a more profound, less obvious level. They claim that it liberates them from the awful consequence of sin, including spiritual death.

So, properly understood, Christian discipleship is not a path of grim duty (although, of course, discipline and duty have their place). Rather it is our joyful, grateful response to someone who has saved and rescued us. At the same time, the death of Jesus – like that soldier's death – challenges and inspires us. We know that our gratitude must be expressed in our lives as well as with our lips. The only proper response to it is to mould our attitudes and actions upon the selfless attitude shown by Jesus in dying for us. This is what is meant by New Testament phrases like 'dying with Christ'.

It means 'putting to death' two desires deep within us. The first desire is to live for comfort and pleasure – to enthrone ourselves at the centre of our own personal universe. How tempting it is to settle for one central aim in life – to make each year more comfortable or exciting than the one before. The second desire is for security. We play safe. By nature and by instinct we want to hold on to what we have. In particular we want to hold on to *ourselves*, for we know that if we are too open to others we are likely to get hurt. So we are cautious. We keep our inner selves under wraps, and refuse to take risks.

Jesus' teaching challenges this attitude. He demands that we should be converted and become like little children. Two qualities displayed by young children are simple trust and *openness*. We must not be sentimental. I don't think for one moment that Jesus was suggesting that little children are always lovely. They can be extremely selfish. They can enjoy bullying and telling tales. But they are *open*.

One morning each week I teach a class of infants and I am struck by their willingness to confide. They will share the things that are on their minds, however trivial, without a trace of embarrassment. They do not have a veneer of sophistication to protect them. But, of course, openness makes them vulnerable. From time to time they get hurt; and so they gradually learn 'wiser' ways – often from adults.

Jesus' teaching challenges us to revert to the greater openness to one another which we knew as children. His death does the same: it challenges our instinct and desire for security and self-protection. If you hold on to yourself, and refuse to take the risks involved in sharing yourself, you will not get hurt. Instead, something worse will happen. You will shrivel up inside. That was the teaching of Jesus and he expressed it vividly in relation to his crucifixion: 'If anyone would come after me, he must deny himself and take up his cross daily and follow me. For whoever wants to save his life will lose it, but whoever loses his life for me will save it' (Luke 9:23–4).

If they are true, these words are very frightening. For they make it clear that we all have to choose between two kinds of death. The fundamental difference between them is this: *only one kind of death leads on to resurrection*. The other leads to the greyness of self-centredness: the sort of 'death' displayed so clearly by some characters in Dickens' novels and in modern soap operas. So, in a sense, there is only one 'Thou shalt not . . .' in the Christian life. 'Thou shalt not live unto thyself.'

A significant difference

Central to this chapter have been the strong parallels between the voluntary death of a soldier and the voluntary death of Jesus. For each of them 'laid down his life for his friends.' In closing, we note one significant *difference* between these two acts of self-sacrifice.

After his death that soldier could do nothing more for his friends. True, the memory of his heroic self-sacrifice lived on powerfully in their imaginations, and it continued to inspire and to challenge. The death of Jesus works in that way, too. But at the heart of the Christian faith is the affirmation that Jesus lives on, not only in our memories, but *by his actual presence*.

Before he died, Jesus explained to his puzzled disciples that it would be good for them if he were to die and depart. He went on to tell them that if he went away, he would send another counsellor (or comforter). In other words, he would return to them by his Spirit – and in this way he would be present everywhere, in every age. He would not be limited to one locality, or to one generation.

Now the Holy Spirit, the Spirit of Jesus, and the Counsellor are different New Testament terms for one central reality. That reality is the continuing presence of Jesus with, and within, his followers. So, in addition to leaving an inspiring and challenging example to work in our memories, *Jesus himself* lives within us by his Spirit. How greatly we need him! For we need something more than inspiration and direction – important as these are. We need help and strength, too.

Archbishop William Temple put it like this, in a memorable illustration.

> It is no good giving me a play like *Hamlet* or *King Lear*, and telling me to write a play like that. Shakespeare could do it; I can't. And it is no good showing me a life like the life of Jesus, and telling me to live a life like that. Jesus could do it; I can't. But if the genius of Shakespeare could come and live in me, then I could write plays like that. And if the Spirit of Jesus could come and live in me, then I could live a life like that.

But that is a big claim and it raises a big question. *Does it work*? We turn to that next.

POSTSCRIPT

1 *On Anastasis*. Dour words like 'death' and 'crucifixion' are sprinkled generously on the pages of the New Testament. But when we come across them we can be sure that positive words like 'resurrection' and 'life' won't be far away. In the Acts of the Apostles, there is an interesting passage which underlines the strong connection between Jesus and *life*. St Paul found his way to a public debating area in intellectual Athens – a kind of up-market Hyde Park Corner. 'What is this babbler trying to say?' asked some philosophers. Their friends replied, 'He seems to be advocating foreign gods' (Acts 17:18). Note: *gods* not *god*.

We soon discover why they used the plural – it was because Paul was preaching the good news about Jesus and the resurrection. The Greek word for resurrection is *anastasis*, and because Jesus and resurrection are so clearly linked together, those who half-heard thought that Paul was talking about a god (Jesus) and a goddess (Anastasis)!

2 *On freedom*. I am grateful to my friend David Weekes for drawing my attention to a powerful passage in a book by his one-time history tutor, G. Kitson Clark. Entitled *The*

Kingdom of Free Men, the book ends with these words: 'So we have reached the end of our journey, and we have arrived at no pleasant place. It is in fact a place of public execution. Yet all human roads lead here in the end. This is the capital of the kingdom of free men and there, ruling from the gallows, is the King.'

This moving insight finds support from many Bible passages – especially St John's Gospel where the death of Jesus is shown to be his glory, too. But the quotation has one possible drawback – a drawback perhaps shared with the powerful symbol of the crucifix, when compared with an empty cross. For Jesus rules from the gallows, because he rose from the dead.

3 *Life from death.* 'The blood of the martyrs is the seed of the Church.' Tertullian's phrase has often been confirmed – for the life of the Church has often been renewed by persecution courageously faced. During the last war, priests from a town in Papua New Guinea, were captured and escorted to a beach. They were told that they would remain safe provided they did not practise their faith. Those men refused to compromise and were executed on the spot. Even today, that small town in that vast diocese provides nearly half of the candidates required for ordained ministry within the Church.

Reflecting on this, Bishop Peter Ball drew a sharp lesson. 'Many churches today call their members not to sacrifice, but to "involvement", to superficial study, cosy prayer and church business. This is not life-changing.'

9

TRANSFORMING GOD

We ended the last chapter with a big claim and an important question. The claim was that the Spirit of Jesus is alive and active in our world, and that he is able to transform his followers into the likeness of Jesus himself. The inevitable question is: Does it work? Which is another way of asking: Is Christianity true? For the Christian faith stands or falls with the claim that Jesus rose from the dead and is alive and active today.

Now it would be an arrogant and foolish Christian who would say: 'Yes it does work,' without qualification. Many people have said – and with some justification – that they cannot believe in Jesus as Saviour, because they see so little evidence of people in the Church actually being saved. Which is another way of saying that too many Christians remain self-centred in action, and limited in vision. Indeed, I feel the force of this objection so strongly, that I wish to modify Archbishop William Temple's illustration, with which we ended the previous chapter. For while it carries force, it overstates the case.

Imagine for a moment that the impossible *did* happen, and that the genius of Shakespeare could somehow come to live within me. Unless he took over completely and obliterated my personality altogether, his genius would be obstructed by my limited powers. He would be hampered by my lack of imagination; by my inability to concentrate; and by a thousand other things. With his help my plays might be good: I doubt that they would ever be great.

In the same way, when the Spirit of Jesus lives within us, he chooses to work with the raw material presented to him. It is *him and me together*, not just 'him'. If he intends to produce a life anything like that of the earthly Jesus, while using the imperfect materials which I present to him, he is in for a great deal of patient work. *For salvation is not a theoretical doctrine*. It is very concrete. It means allowing God to get to work on my bad temper, on my irritability, on my greed, on my thoughtlessness, on my . . .

Sometimes, with some people, he does not seem to make any progress at all – which was the point St Paul made when he roundly asserted that 'if a man does not possess the Spirit of Christ, he is no Christian' (Rom. 8:9 NEB). It is possible to be a church-goer, and it is possible to lead a passably upright moral life without the Spirit of Christ within us. 'By their fruit you will recognise them' (Matt. 7:16), said Jesus. And the harvest he looks for goes well beyond passable morality and decency. For the fruit of God's Spirit in human lives is 'love, joy, peace, patience, kindness, goodness, faithfulness, gentleness and self-control' (Gal. 5:22–3).

But . . . no judgment of other people, please. We have quite enough to do – co-operating with the Spirit of Jesus in cultivating this fruit in our own lives – without spending time harshly judging other people. Of course, it is possible to be an interested observer of church life without being a harsh critic. I am the former; I hope I am not the latter. On the basis of my observations I would claim that, when every allowance has been made for the many failings of the followers of Jesus, we *can* discern the transforming work of God in people's lives. Below, I set out some of the evidence on which this assertion is based.

1 The transformation of individual lives

Then . . . Throughout the history of the Church there have been many individuals with a powerful 'before and after' story. Saul met Jesus on the Damascus Road and he was transformed – but not transformed out of sight. St Paul was still recognisable as Saul, the persecutor of Christians, in some regards. His sharp mind and deep learning; his strong but impatient leadership; his restless energy. All these characterised Saul as well as Paul. He demonstrates the truth of John Donne's observation, 'Men do not change their passions: only the objects of them.'

St Augustine is another famous example. He wrestled with his sexuality and with conflicting ideas. 'Is Christianity true?' and 'How can I control my passions?' These were Augustine's questions, and the solution to both came to him in a friend's garden in Milan in AD 386. Augustine heard a young child singing these words: 'Take up and read, take up and read.' Augustine did just that. He picked up a copy of St Paul's letter to the Romans and he read, 'not in orgies and drunkenness, not in sexual immorality and debauchery, not in dissension and jealousy. Rather, clothe yourselves with the Lord Jesus Christ, and do not think about how to gratify the desires of the sinful nature' (Rom. 13:13–14).

In that instant he found his answer. It transformed him. And because he was so influential, it transformed a fair bit of history, too. As he reflected upon that moment he wrote, 'No further would I read, nor had I any need; instantly, at the end of this sentence, a clear light flooded my heart and all the darkness of doubt vanished away.'

. . . and now. This kind of dramatic conversion still happens, and many books of biography and autobiography bear witness to this fact.[1] In addition to those who become famous, many unknown Christians can tell a similar story, and I shall sketch a few details about some of these.

Over the past few months I have travelled widely and met a large number of people. Three girls stand out. They do not know each other and they live miles apart – but each told a similar story. They were on drugs. To feed their habit they became ruthless and resorted to theft. One described herself as a 'con girl'. She specialised in getting wealthy 'good-time men' to take her to their homes. She would ensure that they drank a lot, while she kept a clear head. Then she would ransack the houses for valuables.

As we talked it was difficult to recognise the people they were describing – for these girls appeared to be caring, concerned and honest. People who knew them well vouched for them, and I did not doubt their stories – which

---

[1] For example, *Comeback*, by the actor James Fox (Hodder 1983). Also: books by and about Fred Lemon, a converted criminal (Marshall Morgan & Scott).

were told with sincerity and integrity, and without embellishment or pride. They reminded me of a description I once heard of a man who underwent a Christian conversion: 'It is the same skin, but with a different man inside!' The past has not completely lost its power over those girls. For example, one of them told me about bad dreams from her past life which continue to disturb her. But the transformation of their personalities is striking.

One thing is clear. The revolution in their lives cannot be accounted for in terms of 'turning over a new leaf' or 'pulling themselves together'. They had neither the moral vision nor the spiritual strength to achieve such a radical change. Something happened *to* them.

In the New Testament letter to the Ephesians we find this remarkable line: 'He who has been stealing must steal no longer, but must work . . . that he may have something to share with those in need' (4:28). It is stated without amplification or surprise. Now scholars tell us that *Ephesians* was probably a circular letter. So it looks as though the power of the Gospel to transform was so great that converted thieves were to be found in many congregations. It is a throw-away remark – but extremely revealing. It takes us back to the Gospels, where we find Jesus inviting Zaccheus the crook to become a disciple, and declaring that he has come to seek and to save the lost.

I know of several men who have been lively Christians for many years now, having spent time in prison for various crimes. So the Church in our day is not totally different from the early Church in this regard. For such people, the strong New Testament teaching that we have passed from death to life, and from darkness to light, makes a lot of sense. As does that vivid assertion that 'if anyone is in Christ, he is a new creation' (2 Cor. 5:17).

Of course, dramatic stores of personal transformation occur in contexts other than a life of crime. A friend of mine is in great demand as a leader of retreats, for he is a skilful teacher of contemplative prayer. He was introduced to the Christian faith when, as a young man, his life was 'in a mess' (his own words). He knew that he desperately needed inner strength and stillness. And he found these qualities – and

the transforming love of God as well – in the practice of prayer, and in silence. This is not escapism: he lives a very busy life and has to make a determined effort to find space for quietness.[2]

Ordinary people. But what about those people in our churches – probably the large majority – who don't have such a black-and-white experience? Does the Gospel have anything to offer them, too? Yes! The Gospel is still the power of God, and it is always about transformation – whether our background is upright and respectable or devious and crooked.

Last year I came to know a student who had recently become a Christian. He was a quiet man: gentle, respectable and private. Before his Christian conversion he was a very pleasant person and a model citizen. Certainly this man was no thief! But he, too, has been changed – albeit in less dramatic ways.

Before his newly-found faith he lived his life in as 'safe' an environment as possible: mainly in the company of a small group of trusted friends. When he came to faith in Christ, it was a great joy to see him gradually becoming a broader person with wider interests. He was prepared to

---

[2]I strongly recommend his recent book: *Contemplating the Word*, Peter Dodson (SPCK, 1987).

take risks, to relate to a wider circle of people, and to be involved in demanding activities which were not 'safe' (like talking about his new-found faith in the Students' Union!). He began to see life in terms of love, service, and discipleship, rather than safety and security. He even considered working abroad – something which would have been impossible before, given his 'play-it-safe' policy.

2 Transformation of communities
Time-honoured customs can be the foundation of a strong culture. But customs sometimes stand in the way of progress and compassion. 'The way we do things here' is not always a recipe for healthy growth – a truth which is sometimes sadly illustrated within churches. Life often demands change, as the following example shows.

The Masai people in Kenya built a dam. In 1976 it burst and all their precious water was lost. Rice powder was flown in to prevent starvation. According to Masai custom, old people are given food; young people find their own. A crisis developed. Then an evangelist explained the teaching of the Bible – God loves everyone, old and young alike. The elders considered this and agreed that the food should be shared with the young people, too. A simple but clear illustration of the fact that the outlook of entire communities can be transformed by the Christian Gospel.

Dramatic . . . Another powerful example of this is found in the book referred to in the previous chapter *(Miracle on the River Kwai)*. In a chapter entitled 'Church Without Walls', Ernest Gordon describes how a new spirit spread through some of the prisoner-of-war camps. This followed a few radiant examples of self-sacrifice, and the rediscovery of the teaching of Jesus. As a result of reflecting upon all that had happened, he wrote:

So far as many of us could see, there were three definitions of the Church. There was the church composed of laws, practices, pews, pulpits, stones and steeples; the church adorned with the paraphernalia of state. Then there was the church composed of creeds and catechisms, where it was identified only by words.

Finally there was the Church of the Spirit, called out of the world to exist in it by reason of its joyful response to the initiative of God's love. Such a church had the atmosphere not of law court nor of classroom but of divine humanity. It existed wherever Christ's love burned in the heart of man. The physical temple and the doctrinal affirmation are both necessary to the fullness of the Church – but both are dead without the church that is communion, the fellowship of God's people.

. . . and undramatic. As with individuals, so with communities. It is not just in dramatic situations that the power of God to transform is experienced. It also happens to ordinary communities, in ordinary situations. Recently I spoke with a curate from a church which I know fairly well. I knew that one of his predecessors had been unhappy in that job. Rightly or wrongly, that earlier curate had felt pressurised and undervalued. When I asked his successor how he was getting on he replied: 'I am very happy here; they are a very loving congregation.'

Of course, some of the more difficult members may have moved away. In any case, the first curate may have been partly to blame for his own unhappiness. But when every allowance had been made for these factors, it was clear to me as I mingled with the people and spoke to the curate that a genuine transformation had come over that congregation. A change for the better.

None of the above amounts to proof for the existence of a transforming God. They are nothing more than illustrations and examples offered for consideration. Whether we find them convincing or not will depend to some extent upon our own personal experience. Perhaps we have seen too many churches which are strong on words, but light on deeds. Or – even worse – we may have met people who appear to be *less* interesting and 'rounded' as a result of Christian conversion. Perhaps their lives are now lived entirely within a Christian cocoon – in which a round of cosy meetings acts as insulation against face-to-face contact with a needy world.

Certainly I am aware of some negative examples of this kind. Nevertheless, I have been fortunate enough to enjoy many positive encounters which convince me of the genuine activity of God in the lives of individuals and communities. I remain convinced that these transformations are the work of God's Spirit and are not to be explained entirely in psychological terms. (Although, of course, our minds and emotions are strongly involved in any fundamental change. So there *is* a psychology of conversion – and it is quite proper for Christians to study it, and contribute to it.)

Personal. In part, my conviction is based on observation – for I have been privileged to watch several radically-changed individuals withstand various pressures over many years. I am impressed by the wide range of personality types – they are not all naturally 'religious people' by any means. My conviction also springs from my own personal experience *of myself*. Sometimes it seems possible to 'stand outside' ourselves, and almost to become objective spectators of our own lives. When I do this, I am aware of very powerful changes in my own outlook and attitudes. These seem to have been brought about within me by an external source of energy. Of course I am involved – but as *co-operator* not initiator.

For example, when I became a convinced Christian in my early twenties, I became aware for the first time of the needs of the elderly. Until that moment I had more or less ignored their existence. But after my conversion, I started visiting elderly people and made several good friends.

I don't say this boastfully; indeed, I received much more *from* them than I gave *to* them. I now see just how kindly they were in allowing me to practise my pastoral skills on them! But it is relevant to record this fact, for as I reflect upon that experience, I believe that God was changing me. He was opening my eyes to the needs of other people; encouraging me to serve; broadening my vision and my interests. With regret, I confess that in some ways I have gone backwards ever since. Inadequate and clumsy as I was, I was aware of being made more loving and concerned. I can only describe it by saying that something was being done *to* me, and *with* me, by another. Or rather, *by Another*. By the God who transforms.

3 The transformation of words

Shortly after the death of Jesus, the world saw a remarkable release of creative, joyful energy. This led to a new form of literature (the Gospels); to a new form of community (the sharing Church); ultimately to a new form of book (the codex with a spine rather than a scroll); to transformed people; and to new and enriched words and concepts.

The most celebrated example of the latter is . . . love (which in the Bible is a *five*-letter word). Greek, the language of the New Testament, is rich in words for love: philia (deep friendship); storge (family affection); eros (sexual love). But these words were already packed with meaning, so when the New Testament writers wanted to talk about love – as they often did – they selected another word: *Agape*. They did not invent the word, but they did transform it.

At the time of Jesus there were many Jewish communities outside Palestine. They were to be found in pretty well every town around the Mediterranean, and like most other people they spoke Greek. To enable these communities to study the Scriptures (our Old Testament), a Greek translation from the Hebrew had been completed around the year 250 BC. It is called the Septuagint, and in that translation we occasionally find the word *agape*. It meant 'love', but it was much less famous and rich in meaning than words like eros and philia.

The New Testament writers took that word and baptised it into Christ. They poured into it a new content, for they took as its basis the life and death of Jesus. In this way they transformed it from a rather colourless word, into the most beautiful single word in all human speech.

You may never learn New Testament Greek. But I hope that as a result of this book, you will have one word in your Greek vocabulary.[3] That single word is AGAPE (each

---

[3] I hope you will also have one Aramaic word in your vocabulary (see Chapter 5).

letter is pronounced). Its importance has been recognised by some people who do not accept the Christian faith. Bertrand Russell, for example. Although he was not a Christian, he asked:

> What stands in the way of true progress? Not physical or technical obstacles, but only the evil passions in human minds; suspicion, fear, lust for power, intolerance . . . The root of the matter is a very simple and old-fashioned thing, a thing so simple that I am almost ashamed to mention it, for fear of the derisive smile with which wise cynics will greet my words. The thing I mean – please forgive me for mentioning it – is love, Christian love, or compassion . . .

POSTSCRIPT

1 *On love*. In the middle of St Paul's great hymn on the subject of love (1 Cor. 13) we come across a severely practical list. The world will be a better place if we memorise it and attempt to act upon it, with God's help. 'Love is patient, love is kind. It does not envy, it does not boast, it is not proud. It is not rude, it is not self-seeking, it is not easily angered, it keeps no record of wrongs. Love does not delight in evil but rejoices with the truth. It always protects, always trusts, always hopes, always perseveres. Love never fails' (1 Cor. 13:4–8).

These verses make it clear that *agape* is a very practical quality – more a matter of the will than of the emotions. Which reminds me of two other memorable statements on love. The first is by William Blake, the great visionary artist who wrote the famous poem, 'Jerusalem'. 'He who would do good to another must do it in Minute Particulars.' The second is from a book on psychology whose title and author I have forgotten. It included a statement about the importance of love in human relationships, which it defined as a thousand acts of kindness, courtesy and thoughtfulness.

2 *On Conversion*. David L. Edwards, now Provost of Southwark Cathedral, wrote:

> That is why everyone is challenged to respond to God through Jesus Christ in a *personal turning* (which is what the word 'conversion' means). You have to meet Jesus yourself, and to accept him as your friend and as your Lord . . . In the Church of England's new Baptism service, a question is put. It is very simple, but very searching. 'Do you turn to Christ?' . . . To turn to Christ is to turn to the Liberator.
>
> In many Christian lives, this turning or conversion reaches a climax which can be dated. People can remember the exact time when they accepted Jesus Christ as Lord and Liberator, often after intense struggles to escape from the pressure of his love. But it is not necessary to be able to date your conversion like that.
>
> What is essential is that everyone should have his or her personal reasons for being a Christian. You cannot inherit Christian faith as you can inherit red hair or a peculiar nose. You cannot copy Christian faith as you can copy hairstyle or an accent. And you cannot get it completely out of books, as you can get a knowledge of history. Your faith, to be authentic, to guide your life, must be your own. Your very own experience, whether it is dramatic or quiet, long or short, must lead you to know Jesus Christ as your personal Liberator (*What Anglicans Believe*, Mowbray, 1974).

10

DEMANDING GOD

Klaus Klostermaier was a missionary in India. He wrote a moving and perceptive book about his experiences, entitled *Hindu and Christian in Vrindaban* (SCM, 1969). One incident concerns an elderly Hindu woman, who undertook a long and arduous pilgrimage in the most rigorous possible way.

> On a particular spot of the route, 108 pebbles had to be collected and then moved . . . pebble by pebble, the length of the body at a time. After all 108 pebbles have been moved the distance of about two steps, one starts all over again. How long does it take to make a pilgrimage in this manner? Weeks – perhaps months . . . Weeks later I saw her (the widow) still at it, a few kilometres ahead of the spot where we had first discovered her. She seemed so weak that after every twenty metres, she remained lying exhausted next to her small pile of stones.

Klaus Klostermaier's Hindu guide suggested that the woman probably undertook the pilgrimage in this way to earn extra merit for her dead husband. In an earlier chapter I suggested that belief in the Score-card God can lead to despair or to pride. Clearly, such a belief can also lead to acts of enormous heroism.

On reading that episode I reacted in two ways. I felt deeply moved and challenged by that old woman's courage and persistence – which arose, I suspect, from a mixture of love, despair and grief. And I longed that someone would lift her gently from the dust and read to her these lovely words of Jesus: 'Come to me, all you who are weary and burdened, and I will give you rest. Take my yoke upon you and learn from me, for I am gentle and humble in heart, and you will find rest for your souls. For my yoke is easy and my burden is light' (Matt. 11:28–30).

Many religious people, including some who stand within the Christian tradition, think of God as that elderly Hindu widow did – although few people in the West work out their beliefs as rigorously. On this view, religion is a matter of living in such a way that God will be pleased with us. If we do so, he will bestow his favours upon me, including the ultimate favour of heaven.

As we have seen (Chapter 2), the Christian Gospel is radically different from this. Indeed, it turns this approach on its head. For Christian ethics and behaviour are not based on 'work and earn' but on 'receive and respond'. God's love is so great that he has *already* showered his good gifts upon us, regardless of our response. As Jesus put it, the sun shines upon the righteous *and* upon the unrighteous, without distinction. There is no question of our *persuading* him to be on our side. He has already proved that he is, in the most dramatic way possible: by sending his Son to us and for us.

We cannot earn God's favours. They are free; there for the taking. Preachers and theologians sometimes express this truth by saying that God's love is 'unconditional'. But this is not quite accurate. For gifts must be accepted and received. To force someone to receive a gift is to do violence to the very notion of giving and receiving. Imagine a rich aunt who writes to a neglectful nephew and asks him to visit her because she wants to give him a present. The nephew has certainly not earned the gift – indeed he deserves nothing at all from his elderly aunt, whom he ignores. She loves him just the same, and to benefit from her love he must do one simple thing. For unless he stirs himself to receive the gift, it will not be his.

We are rather like that nephew in our relationship to God. Except that we cannot carry his gifts away in our hands. We can only carry them in our hearts and in our lives. He has two gifts for us. First, he wants to give us *himself*. Second, he wants to give us *ourselves* too – ourselves, with all our potential fulfilled. The first he does in many ways: by the bread and wine in Holy Communion, by the gift of the teaching of his Son, and by the gift of his

Holy Spirit in our lives, for example. The second he does by
accepting our offering of ourselves to him, and then hand-
ing it back to us. In the process (a long one) he remakes and
restores us.

To put this another way, God requires the same generous
self-giving spirit *from* us, as that which he shows *to* us. He
loves us, and we accept and receive his love by our willingness to love him – and by our willingness to make this
concrete by loving other people. This is a very tall order,
but all that he requires from us is our *willingness*. He
promises all the help we shall need; and when we fail, he
promises forgiveness, too. We don't have to succeed; we
do need to be willing to allow him to change us in the
process of trying.

These ideas are hard to grasp in an abstract form, so I will
give some key examples of what is involved in being
receptive to God's gifts, drawn from the teaching of Jesus.
He summed it up at the beginning of his ministry when he
said, 'The kingdom of God is near. Repent and believe the
good news!' (Mark 1:15). To repent means to turn round;
to develop a new attitude – a completely new way of
looking at life and relationships. The phrase 'kingdom of
God' indicates the direction of the required change. Jesus
stressed three qualities in particular.

1   We must give

Jesus encourages us to be relaxed about our possessions.
They are on loan for a mere seventy years or so, so it is
foolish to get too attached to them, or to build our security
upon them. In particular, we are called to help the poor. By
giving we achieve two things. First, we help those in need.
In this regard we are to *think small*. We may not be able to
solve the world's economic problems; we *can* provide food
for a few empty bellies and shoes for a few bare feet.
Second, we help ourselves. For the less we depend upon
our possessions, the more we learn to trust God. This was
an important emphasis in the teaching of Jesus, and we
shall return to it in Chapters 11 and 12.

2 We must forgive

On Remembrance Sunday, 1987, an IRA bomb caused death and destruction in the town of Enniskillen in Northern Ireland. The behaviour of those caught up in the horror was inspiring, and the Queen referred to this in her speech to the Commonwealth on Christmas Day, 1987.

> From time to time we also see some inspiring examples of tolerance. Mr Gordon Wilson, whose daughter Marie lost her life in the horrifying explosion at Enniskillen on Remembrance Sunday, impressed the world by the depth of his forgiveness. His strength, and that of his wife, and the courage of their daughter came from their Christian convictions. All of us will echo their prayer that out of the personal tragedies of Enniskillen may come reconciliation between the communities.

This reminds us that forgiveness is strong, not weak. It is the one quality which is needed to stop the cycle of violence in so many of the world's trouble spots (which too often turn into horror spots). Of course, it is not easy – even on the domestic level. When everything is going well within my family, kind deeds are simple. When my children are thoughtful, it is a real pleasure for me to be helpful – to give them lifts in the car, or to make cups of tea to keep them going with their homework. But if we have a row, all that changes. I don't want to be helpful. Instead I want to nurse my emotional bruises and to expend my energy on justifying myself.

Now forgiveness does not mean that I must attempt to manufacture warm, cosy thoughts on such occasions. It is more a matter of the will than of the emotions. It involves me in attempting to do the best for them, even though I don't *feel* like doing so.

Sixteenth century. One clear example of this comes from the life of the sixteenth-century Jesuit, Edmund Campion. He lived in England when it was extremely dangerous to be an active Roman Catholic priest, and he worked hard to sustain the faith of those who shared his convictions. But eventually he was betrayed, tortured and condemned to death.

One day he received a remarkable visitor in his condemned cell – the man who had betrayed him. Would Father Campion forgive him? Yes. Would Father Campion help him to escape, for his life was in constant danger? So Edmund Campion, weak and in pain from the rack, promised to introduce the man to a nobleman friend in Germany. His betrayer escaped. Edmund Campion was hanged, drawn and quartered.

This brings us right into the centre of the teaching of Jesus. 'Love your enemies' (Luke 6:27). The country in which he announced this absurd instruction was occupied by a hostile power. Jesus was not starry-eyed and sentimental, for he lived in a harsh and brutal world. I doubt that Edmund Campion felt nice warm thoughts towards his betrayer. He was not required to do so. Jesus' teaching on forgiveness and love required him to *act* with the man's best possible interests in mind, whatever his personal feelings. Again, we see that forgiveness is more a matter of the mind and will than of emotions and feelings.

We see, too, that Christian love works on a different principle from most other kinds of love. Love often works on the *magnet* principle: something attractive in the other person 'draws out' a generous response. Christian love and forgiveness work on the *engine* principle. This principle was illustrated by St Francis of Assisi. Fuelled by his love for Christ, he overcame his lifelong fear of leprosy by kissing and embracing a leprosy sufferer. Like him, we are called to love people whom we find *un*attractive – even an enemy or betrayer. Most of us can do this only when God pours his love into our hearts, and when Jesus' teaching and example grip and fire our imagination.

Twentieth century. None of this leads to slushy sentimentality or pretence. Geoffrey Prime was imprisoned for abusing children and for spying. His espionage came to light because his wife believed that she should tell the police. But she continues to love her husband. She visits him in prison and patiently awaits his release – a long wait, probably into the next century.

Many people in the modern world do not understand Jesus' teaching about forgiveness at a deep level, because our lives are comfortable and insulated, and we don't have many enemies. Jesus lived in a country occupied by tough soldiers. Most of us don't, thank God. But our situation can give us a false sense of our own goodness.

I recall speaking to a young man with a warm, outgoing personality. In twenty-two years he had never experienced any problems with forgiveness, and he thought this was because he understood and accepted the teaching of Jesus. In fact, it was because he had never been tested. One day his girlfriend of long-standing jilted him and went out with another boy, right under his nose. The jilted man found all kinds of unpleasant emotions at work within him – emotions like anger, bitterness and a desire for revenge. He had great difficulties with forgiveness. Eventually he came through that crisis much wiser and stronger.

On being hurt, some people struggle with deep emotions for many years. More than once I have heard people utter that most terrible phrase: 'I can never forgive him.' We may not condone this, but we can understand – and pray that Jesus will do his strong, patient work in their lives.

The strength and power of forgiveness can be immense. Ruby Bridges, a 6-year-old black child, was caught up in the struggle for civil rights in New Orleans in 1960. For weeks she was the only child to attend her school. Every day she walked through jeering white crowds, who refused to allow their children to attend the same school. She got through because she was escorted by US marshals. Robert Coles, a child psychiatrist who won the Pulitzer Prize, noticed that Ruby talked to herself as she walked through the hostile crowd. He asked her what she was saying, and she told him that she was praying. 'What did you say in your prayer?' he asked. Ruby replied, 'I prayed like Jesus, forgive them for they don't know what they are doing'.

Donald Shriver, who records this in *Forgiveness and Politics* (1987), adds this comment: '. . . the striking thing about this true incident is not only that Ruby – the child of two illiterate black parents who know the Bible from going to church – prayed as she did; but that Robert Coles, a distinguished American intellectual, is so overwhelmed by her story.'

3 We must not judge

Jesus was very hot on this. God treats us with immense generosity, understanding and forgiveness. We, in turn, must do the same to other people. 'Why do you look at the speck of sawdust in your brother's eye and pay no attention to the plank in your own eye?' (Matt. 7:3). Most of us are rather better at discerning other people's faults than our own. But we have no clear way of knowing what other people's motives are, or what problems they contend with. I recall a man who got annoyed with a colleague who always arrived for work at the last minute. Some months later he discovered that she called on an elderly man each morning to help him wash and dress.

Only God knows the true situation in our lives, including the basic material of our personality and upbringing – the 'raw material' given to us, with which we have to work. If we insist on judging other people, there is ample opportunity for error, as the following incident shows . . .

A pinch in a lift. Some relatives of mine were in a crowded lift. Everyone was behaving as British people should in crowded lifts, and a deep meditative silence descended on the group. But the peace was abruptly disturbed by a tall woman who slapped a mild-looking middle-aged man sharply across the face. She glowered at him, and he went very red. Before this interesting situation could develop further, the lift stopped and everyone piled out. When they dispersed, Jeremy (aged 7) said crossly to his parents: 'That nasty woman stood on my toe, so I pinched her bottom.'

Shortly afterwards, I was in conversation with a friend about a colleague who was on the receiving end of some serious accusations – not pinching bottoms I hasten to add. I gladly believed my colleague's protestations of innocence, and so did my friend. Now this friend is a wise man, and he went on to say that those false accusations gave the lie once again to the most misleading proverb in the English language. (Now there's a poser for you: which of our many English proverbs qualifies for *that* particularly undistinguished title?)

He was quite clear. In his view, the most mischievous of all our proverbs is: 'There's no smoke without fire.' For it suggests that every rumour contains *some* truth – and a moment's thought shows this to be quite false. But it's a moment we don't often bother to find – so we play into the hands of every slanderer, every gossip and every scandal-monger who enjoys destroying reputations.

Many Bible passages contradict that dangerous proverb, and I'll leave you with two. The first is from the ten commandments. 'You shall not bear false witness,' declares number nine. And then – perhaps most nerve-racking of all – there are the words of Jesus in the Sermon on the Mount: 'Do not judge, or you too will be judged. For in the same way as you judge others, you will be judged, and with the measure you use, it will be measured to you' (Matt. 7:1–2).

Jesus does not offer this as 'food for thought'. His statement comes as a command from our Demanding God. It is not open to negotiation. For if we refuse to give and to forgive, and if we insist on judging harshly, our hearts and lives are firmly closed against God – so tightly closed that we cannot receive his gifts. As the Lord's Prayer makes disturbingly clear: no forgiveness *from* us, means no forgiveness *for* us.

It isn't easy. But all the help that we need is there for the asking.

POSTSCRIPT

1 *Dying for him*. Sometimes Jesus makes heavy demands with a light touch. More than once he refers to the possibility that his disciples might be persecuted for their faith. Don't worry about your enemies, he says. Why, the worst they can do is to kill you. Don't fear men; fear God instead (Luke 12:1–7). He sometimes views death as a little hiccup along the continuing line of our eternal existence.

Some have taken this teaching with the utmost seriousness. The Ugandan martyrs for example. In October 1984, shortly after several young men had become disciples of Jesus, an 18-year-old called Mwanga assumed leadership of their tribe. He made it clear that those young men must choose between following him and following Christ. They chose Christ. As a result, many of them were burned to death over a slow fire. All who saw them die spoke of their courage and serenity.

Bishop Stephen Neill – an outstanding and widely-travelled Christian leader of our century – found the martyrs' cross which marked their heroism to be the most moving place on earth. When he told the local bishop how he felt, he replied, 'If it came to it, I think the Baganda would be ready to die for Christ today; it is living for him that they find difficult.'

2   *Living for him.* I visited my parents and looked out of their window. My mother waved at a passing neighbour, and said, 'That woman is a saint.' I expressed interest, and my mother told me that June's adult son and daughter-in-law had been attacked and brutally killed in their own home. In the midst of the horror, the grief and the tears, June looked sad and thoughtful, and someone asked what was on her mind. She replied that she was thinking of the murderer's mother. June expressed her deep sorrow for the hurt which *that* mother was suffering as a result of the tragedy, and the subsequent trial of her son. I wondered how many other great saints were about their daily business that Monday morning – unrecognised and unsung by other people in their local shops and streets.

3   *Learning from him.*

Our progress towards God is cyclic, like climbing a spiral staircase. You may find yourself later wanting to return to spending time on prayer for sorrow and repentance because you have reached a deeper level of awareness of God's goodness which reveals areas of unbelief in your life which you have never noticed before (*God of Surprises*, Gerard Hughes, DTL, 1985).

4   *Growing in him.* 'I saw on the walls of Notre-Dame de Paris a notice which stated: "Sin is a refusal to grow bigger." . . . We sin if we refuse to grow into the full people that God intended us to be. We sin if we prefer smallness. In this case small is not beautiful: it is petty. A little

sustained thinking about the pettiness in your life, the smallness of your concern and your horizon, the cosiness of the confinement in which you feel safe, would be a useful approach to confession . . . A Church that was helping its members to grow out of pettiness would certainly deserve the name of Church.' Canon Ian Dunlop, Chancellor of Salisbury Cathedral.

5 *United with him*. Jesus provides us with matchless teaching and a peerless example. But if we are to be transformed 'into his likeness' we need more – much more – than that. We need what the New Testament calls 'union with Christ'. We need Jesus' Spirit within us – empowering, challenging and encouraging. The Anglican monk Harry Williams put it like this:

> Being a Christian means . . . being people in whom his (Jesus') life and character and power are manifest and energised . . . Christian experience is not so much a matter of imitating a leader . . . as accepting and receiving a new quality of life – a life infinitely more profound and dynamic and meaningful than human life without Christ.

11

GOD WHO DISLIKES RELIGION

If the Bible is right, then God dislikes religion. Surprising, but true none-the-less. For example, take this passage from Amos, in which the prophet speaks out in the name of the Lord:

> I hate, I despise your religious feasts;
> I cannot stand your assemblies . . .
> Away with the noise of your songs! . . .
> But let justice roll on like a river,
> righteousness like a never-failing stream!
> (Amos 5:21–4).

That is straightforward and clear, but it is not without its complications. Because, despite that and similar passages, religious acts play a central part in the Old Testament. Indeed, it is often God himself who requires his people to pray, to worship and to offer sacrifices. Some Bible readers see this as a head-on clash between prophet and priest. On this view, there were two conflicting schools of thought in Old Testament times. One school (the priestly) valued sacrifice; the other school (the prophetic) did not. Both viewpoints found their way into the Scriptures: hence the contradiction.

Undoubtedly a tension did sometimes exist, but this is not a very helpful approach, for some prophets had strong links with priests. For example, the famous call of the prophet Isaiah took place inside the Temple (Isa. 6). When we move to the New Testament, Jesus is seen as the fulfilment of the prophetic *and* the priestly traditions. As an example of the former, see Matthew 12:17 on which Chapter 3 is based. The whole of the letter to the Hebrews is an example of the latter. The writer shows that Jesus himself is the one perfect sacrifice *and* the supreme high priest.

An illustration might take us a little further down the road of understanding. It comes from my own undistinguished career as a footballer. We were not much of a team: strong on enthusiasm, but light on goals, alas. One murky November afternoon we were improving our souls by losing yet again. The match was nearly over when one of our midfield players watched the ball pass by. The pitch was muddy and heavy and he could not raise the energy for a hefty kick. In deep anguish our worthy captain called out, 'Don't *look* at the ball.' Now strictly speaking he didn't mean that, for 'keep your eye on the ball' is the first rule for footballers. But we clearly understood his meaning: don't *just* look at the ball; *kick* it as well!

Back to the prophets. This is what Amos means us to understand in the passage quoted at the beginning of this chapter. Don't *just* offer sacrifices – for religious practices are only pleasing to God if they are accompanied by a sacrificial life style. True religion must affect the *whole* of our lives. To practise religion while ignoring God's command to love one another is worse than not being religious at all.

Religion and hypocrisy. To offer sacrifice on the Sabbath, and to ignore widows or exploit orphans during the week, is nothing but hypocrisy. That was the complaint which Amos made over 2,700 years ago, and his words continue to be relevant today. For it still happens. An elderly grocer was telling me about his boyhood. The owner of the shop where he worked was a pillar of the church. He was also harsh and mean. The man who recounted his boyhood experiences is himself a Christian, and he spoke more in sadness than out of bitterness. His deep regret was that the grocer blackened God's name for his employees. 'If that's what being a Christian means, then I don't want anything to do with it.'

Religion has no virtue at all unless it spills over into life. Indeed it can be very dangerous. For it can lead us into those strongest spiritual dangers called pride, hypocrisy, complacency and presumption. (Presuming that God

will forgive me – so why bother? Another term is 'cheap grace'.) It is for this reason that religion is given such a bad write-up in the Bible.

Jesus made it clear that there was more hope for the repentant tax-collector than for the pious but harsh, Pharisee. For every tax-collector knew that he was a crook, but not every Pharisee realised that he was a sinner. Of course, some Pharisees did follow Jesus, and some tax-collectors did not repent, but the point is clear enough. Religion can easily blind us to our own deepest needs. It can mislead us into thinking that we are better than other people. It can persuade me that God is especially pleased with *my* efforts.

One box, not two. Almost every page in the Bible forbids us to divide our lives into two boxes – one labelled 'religious activities'; the other called 'real life'. It is for this reason that Jesus spoke with two voices on the question of religion. On the one hand, he encouraged deep faith in God, and practices like prayer and attendance at the synagogue. On the other hand, he hammered away about the dangers of religion without love and humility. For prayer without these qualities is not real prayer at all.

At bedtime, a mother was listening to her daughter's prayers. The little girl peeped through her fingers and said, 'I'm doing this rather well, aren't I, Mummy?' Perhaps we needn't worry too much when a child speaks like this (although her mother *was* rather shaken!), but sometimes we find the same approach lurking deep within our adult minds. If so, beware!

This theme is taken up elsewhere in the New Testament. For example, James (the brother of Jesus) urges Christians not to become teachers of the faith. Given the need for leaders in the Church, this is rather surprising. But James was concerned for the spiritual welfare of any would-be teachers. For they might feel that their 'up-front' church activities give them a head start over other people. In fact the reverse is true: they will be judged *more* severely. In this regard I recall a sad conversation with an elderly Christian minister. 'I shall die a priest,' he said, with some satisfaction. He seemed to think that this would stand him in good stead on the Day of Judgment. Jesus and James strongly disagree. 'From everyone who has been given much, much will be demanded' (Luke 12:48).

The Victorian Christian Socialist F. D. Maurice summed up the tension between religious activity and real faith when he said: 'We have been dosing our people with religion, when what they want is not this but the living God.' The Jesuit Gerard Hughes makes the same point in *God of Surprises* (DLT, 1985) when he uses this quotation: 'Nothing so masks the face of God as religion.' Which brings us to another, related reason why the Bible is against religion. For even if it doesn't lead to hypocrisy, it can obscure a clear view of God and the Gospel.

Blocking the view. Now I am aware that I am treading on dangerous ground. As a Christian minister I certainly don't want to empty the churches! I believe passionately in the importance of worship, prayer, preaching and sacrament, and I have already emphasised that the Christian faith is not a purely personal, individual matter. 'Me and my God' is cosy but not Christian. Jesus demands *togetherness*. He insists that we relate to one another – and love one another – in the fellowship of the Church.

This is well illustrated by the story of an elderly Scot who stopped attending church. One evening his minister from the Kirk called on him, and they sat either side of the fire in deep silence. Eventually the minister leaned forward, picked up the tongs and removed a red-hot coal from the fire. It gradually became dark and cool. Then he replaced it among the other lumps of coal. Quickly it became hot and bright again, and the whole fire burnt slightly brighter. Then the minister left the cottage. The story has a happy ending. His parishioner took the point, and he was back in church next Sunday.

This simple story illustrates an important truth. *Christians need one another.* But like most parables this tale makes one single point. For it remains true that church can become an end in itself. To pick up F. D. Maurice again, religion can block our view of God. For church-going can lead us into a whirlpool of religious activity instead of pointing us towards the living God, who in turn points us towards a needy world.

There may be no more merit in supporting our local church, than in supporting our local pub. Indeed there may be less merit. For it is possible for Christians to use their local church as a quiet cul-de-sac – a means of getting away from the main highway of life. We meet our friends there; we feel safe and comfortable within its walls; we feel at ease in its activities; we get a sense of significance by sitting on its committees. And because all this is focused on the church, we come to believe that we are deeply spiritual.

If so . . . beware again! Of course, there are times when we need to get away from pressure and noise. Cul-de-sacs can be good places. Of course our faith in God, and our Christian friends, should encourage, support and comfort us. But the teaching of Jesus is *un*comfortable too. He gives us a great command and a great commission. The command is to love; the commission is to spread the Gospel. Both the command and the commission involve us in coming into church in order to go out *from* church – into the rough and tumble of a troubled, divided and sometimes hostile world.

The church that lives to itself – without reaching out in love, and without attempting to share the good news about Jesus – does not deserve to die. *It is dead already.* The Christian whose aim is simply to feed his own spiritual life has lost his way. For there is work to do.

POSTSCRIPT ON DISLIKING CHURCH

After completing this chapter I received a letter from a woman who wrote, 'For about 3 years now, I have become increasingly interested in and aware of Christianity, the pros and cons, etc. Try as I might though, I cannot see any need for attending church . . .'

That woman believes that she can pray in the open air or at home, just as well as in a church building. She is right, of course, in one important sense. For Christianity *is* a personal religion. Each of us must respond personally and individually to the love of God. And we can pray anywhere. But we must not confuse *personal* religion with *private* religion. So I would encourage church membership for several reasons. Here are two.

(a) *Jesus founded the Church*. By this I don't mean that he founded this church or that – but from the beginning he insisted that following him was an exercise in togetherness and fellowship. For as soon as he began his public ministry, he chose a group of twelve people. What a bunch they were! Thomas the timid and Peter the hot-headed for a start. Then there were James and John, the sons of Zebedee. They were greedy for privilege, and it looks as if they were a pretty stormy pair, for they were nicknamed 'Sons of Thunder'. Matthew (or Levi) the tax-collector, and Simon, the Galilean Zealot, were an unlikely pair, too. It must have been very difficult to get them to agree, for one had been a tax-collector who helped the Romans, and the other a freedom fighter. True, Jesus transformed their lives, but they probably sparked each other off from time to time.

Those twelve formed the first Church – because in the New Testament, the word 'Church' refers to a group of people, not to a building. From the start, Jesus was surrounded by sinners. This was brought home to me from the top of a bus. I passed a church with a large notice-board which declared: 'This Church Is For Sinners Only.' Full marks! That notice-board reminds me of the advice sometimes given to new Christians after missions. 'It is important to join a church – but don't go around looking for the perfect church. However, if you *do* find one that is perfect, join it quickly. But remember – as soon as you join it, it will cease to be perfect.'

(b) *Institutions are essential*. Most of us instinctively dislike institutions and bureaucrats – and I well understand why people prefer private religion. But we need to give and receive support, and we can only do this by coming together. Prayer can be private, but worship, sacrament and teaching require us to join with like-minded neighbours. Besides, individuals need institutions to get things done. I recall an elderly woman who worked ceaselessly for leprosy sufferers, and raised large sums of money. This was possible *only* because she worked through churches, which gave out notices and mobilised people-power.

Indeed, I doubt that we should have some of our present excellent helping organisations, were it not for the Church. Samaritans for example. This started in 1953 when the rector of a London church became aware of a large number of despairing people. He set up a telephone listening service which has grown into an international movement. It is not a specifically Christian organisation – help is invited from men and women of all faiths and none. But without a network of churches the idea would have struggled to come alive.

A similar story could be told for Shelter, Christian Aid, and the Hospice Movement. And for Amnesty International too, for this movement was started by a Christian lawyer (literally) on the wings of a prayer.[1] Peter Benenson's vision was for a network of people who would write to prisoners of conscience, and speak on their behalf. His prayer was wonderfully answered, as this recent testimony shows.

---

[1] I am extremely grateful to Peter Benenson, the founder of Amnesty International, for explaining in a personal letter that 'Amnesty was deliberately launched on Trinity Sunday (1961) partly to demonstrate that human suffering was as great in all three parts of our divided world (West, East and Third) and partly to emphasise that the power of the Holy Spirit works to bring together people of diverse origins by inflaming their common conscience.'

When the first two hundred letters came, the guards gave me back my clothes. When the next two hundred letters came, the prison Director came to see me. When the next pile of letters arrived, the Director got in touch with his superior. The letters kept arriving, and the President was informed. The letters still kept arriving, and the President called the prison and told them to let me go.

'Like a mighty tortoise, moves the Church of God,' goes the parody of the hymn – and it is true. But tortoises can move boulders.

12

BIASED GOD

The previous chapter leads on to another subject which is often discussed today, and which Amos raised sharply some 750 years before Christ. Does Amos' stress on justice inevitably lead us into politics? Do politics and faith in God mix? If God strongly dislikes religion without love, does he like politics any better?

This question confronts us from every continent. In South Africa many Christians (black and white) are in the forefront of the struggle against apartheid. Liberation theologians from South and Central America urge Christians to think politically – like Moses who confronted Pharaoh in the name of the Lord. In many countries Christian leaders assert that God is biased towards the poor. In America, born-again Christians claim to speak for the moral majority. In Britain, the Church of England can no longer be called 'the Tory party at prayer', for on many of the big issues we find conflict, tension and confrontation between Church and State. The report entitled *Faith in the City*; the Archbishop of Canterbury and the official service following the Falklands War; the Bishop of Durham's accusation that the Tory government was 'verging on the wicked' when it reorganised the Social Security benefit system, are celebrated examples from the 1980s.

To some the answer is clear. The Christian faith is, or should be, concerned with people's souls. God does not call Christian leaders to get involved in the hurly-burly of politics. Matters of Church and matters of State might overlap from time to time in 'safe' ways – like bishops in the House of Lords, or Presidents being sworn in with Bible in hand. But most of the time, the two spheres should be kept separate.

Others strongly disagree – and their reasons arise from

their understanding of the nature of God, and the nature of politics. The God of the Bible is not a God of religion, nor is he a God of politics. *He is the Lord of all life* – which includes both religion and politics. 'For God so loved *the world*' wrote St John (3:16). Not a little bit of it.

Politics is nothing more and nothing less than the business of organising people in society. Even a cursory interest in world affairs makes it painfully clear that there are good and bad ways of doing this. Alas, more societies seem to be doing it badly than well. Christians cannot avoid being concerned by this, because they believe that the God whom they worship has declared himself *for* just organisation and *against* its mirror image. For justice protects the poor and the powerless. If this is God's point of view, then Christians are called to active involvement in attempting to turn that vision into reality.

Politics in the pulpit? Of course, this does not usually mean that *party* politics should be preached from the pulpit – although this *is* called for in those countries where political parties stand firmly against Christ. For this reason the Confessing Church in Germany opposed the Nazis.

Nor is there a central place for the well-intentioned amateur in the technical fields of (say) economics or defence. For modern politics is complex, and Christian faith does not guarantee technical competence. But there *is* room for the amateur who has reflected long and hard about vital questions like: How should a nation form its priorities? What proportion of its wealth should be spent on defence, on education, on health, on the elderly? Should censorship exist? Should a minority enjoy wealth and rights which are denied to everyone else? How can society give protection and a voice to the powerless? Such questions, which involve compassion, justice and sound judgment, are too important to be left to politicians alone.

Also, there is room for the *local* expert. Church leaders who spend their working lives in one big city, or among farming communities, can speak with authority. They are likely to know more about their local situation than MPs in Whitehall, or Senators in Washington. Their views about local road systems, or local architecture, or local sex shops, or poverty or unemployment, are likely to be well-informed, and highly relevant to the welfare of those among whom they live and work. As the philosopher Sir Karl Popper pointed out: it is easier to centralise power than to centralise the knowledge needed for wise use of that power. Governments often find *that* bit of wisdom very hard to accept.

I am not suggesting that every Christian should be politically active – only that all should be vigilant. But awareness of injustice can catapult a normally non-political person into the political arena. Archbishop Janani Luwum of Uganda wanted nothing more than to preach the Gospel and to pastor his people. But he felt compelled to speak out against Idi Amin's atrocities – and he was shot dead for his trouble.

A New Testament perspective

The New Testament is certainly not a political tract (apart from the Book of Revelation, perhaps). True, it is sometimes said that the early Christians formed a simple communist society. But when political issues are raised by New Testament writers, they are usually dealt with in a moderate manner. Yes, you *should* pay taxes, says Jesus, even when a foreign overlord rules your country. No, slaves should *not* rebel, says Peter. Yes, Christians *should* be good citizens, urges Paul.

But before we conclude that Christians are always called to sit tight and not to rock the boat, we need to dig a little deeper and reflect upon the historical setting. For the Christian Church was a growing but still tiny minority within the apparently all-powerful Roman Empire. The first Christians had enough on their plates in spreading the Gospel, and holding fast to their new faith in a hostile world.

Few of them occupied important positions in society. Most of them were without any political influence at all. So (to take one example) for the early Christians to organise anti-slavery rallies would have been absurd. No tiny group could reorder and reorganise the Roman Empire at such a fundamental level. In any case, many of the early

Christians were themselves slaves, and without vote or voice. The attempt would simply have provided more instant meals for hungry lions.

So they tackled the problem in a different way – by encouraging loyalty, love and mutual responsibility. Christians who were slaves should be good slaves. Christian slave-owners should be kind and considerate. Indeed, they should treat each other as brothers and sisters within a common family. Gentle as this approach might seem, it involved a somersault in outlook and approach. By definition, slaves had no status at all within society. In contrast, the Gospel insisted that slaves had equal status with their owners, for they were children of the same heavenly Father.

Dynamite! Or *derision* more likely. For such an approach was laughable to most Roman citizens. It was the teaching of Jesus which sowed the seeds which eventually led to the outlawing of slavery within Christendom – a step which was far too slow in coming, I readily concede.[1] We should note, too, that the compliant 'good citizen' approach has its limits in the New Testament: there were times when the apostles said a loud 'No' to those in authority. 'Judge for yourselves whether it is right in God's sight to obey you rather than God' (Acts 4:19). But they were prepared to accept the harsh consequences of their civil disobedience – and they never resorted to the spear and the sword.

An Old Testament perspective

In the Old Testament the situation is quite different. Politics and religion overlap almost completely. Even kings were not above the law, for good laws come from God. Those with wealth were to have special regard for the poor and the powerless. This was to be shown in practical, detailed ways. For example, the farmer was forbidden to

---

[1] Professor C.F.D. Moule puts it like this: 'The Christian attitude to slavery placed an explosive charge under the entire institution.' *Sad Footnote*. The Antislavery Society maintains that if we take a global perspective, there are more slaves in the modern world than ever before. They include 'sweat shops' and labour camps in their calculations.

harvest every corner of his field. Some must be left for
widows and orphans.

Above all, the powerful were to ensure that justice
prevailed. Corruption and indifference were common
enough in Israel, but they were against the revealed will of
God, so they never went unchallenged. This was the constant message of the prophets – whose utterances were
often highly political, and sometimes very blunt. They
cover foreign affairs ('trust God') and home affairs ('let
justice reign'). Here is one of the most famous:

> Will the Lord be pleased with
> thousands of rams,
> with ten thousand rivers of oil?
> Shall I offer my firstborn for my transgression,
> the fruit of my body for the sin of my soul?
> He has showed you, O man, what is good.
> And what does the Lord require of you?
> To act justly and to love mercy
> and to walk humbly with your God
>
> (Micah 6:7–8).

Modern prophets
Prophets continue to speak, and I will end this chapter
with two of them. The first is Jim Wallis, leader of the
Sojourner's Community in Washington. In 1986 he toured
Britain and spoke frequently about a 'Bible with holes in'.
He urged Christians to read the Bible *as it actually is* – for
too often we don't 'see' those passages which challenge the
rich, and which speak of God's bias to the poor. In *Call to
Conversion* (Lion, 1981) he writes:

> Not only is the Bible strong in its emphasis; the Scrip-
> tures are stunning in their clarity on this issue. Wealth is
> seen, at best, as a great spiritual danger and, most often,
> as an absolute hindrance to trust in God. The rich are
> continually held responsible for the sufferings of the
> poor, while God is portrayed as the deliverer of the
> oppressed. The God of the Bible has taken sides on this
> matter and has emphatically chosen the side of the poor.

Sharing with the poor is not regarded as an option but as the normal consequences of faith in God.

Archbishop Desmond Tutu is one of the best-known Christians in today's world. Two Indian students gave me a poster with a photo of the archbishop taken while he was preaching. The caption is from one of his sermons: 'I am puzzled about which Bible people are reading, when they suggest religion and politics don't mix.' In *Hammering Swords into Ploughshares* (Ed. I. Mosala: Marshall Pickering, 1987) he takes up this theme again:

In the process of saving the world, of establishing His Kingdom, God, our God, demonstrated that he was no neutral God, but a thoroughly biased God who was forever taking the side of the oppressed, of the weak, of the exploited, of the hungry and homeless, of the refugees, of the scum of society . . . So my dear friends we celebrate, worship and adore our God, the biased God, He who is not neutral, the God who always takes sides.

POSTSCRIPT

1   Dr Frederik Beyers Naudé is the general secretary of the South African Council of Churches. He is a white man with an Afrikaans background, who was brought up to accept apartheid, and to believe in the superiority of the white races. Yet he came to reject those views, and was banned for seven years by the South African government – an action which severely limited his movements.

In *Hope for Faith* (WCC, 1986) he explains the background to his conversion (his word). As a young minister in the Dutch Reformed Church, he studied the Bible and came to the conclusion that the Scriptures point in the opposite direction from apartheid. This led to a personal crisis; for he knew that if he were to speak out, his career would be finished. But he could not pretend to himself – especially as he saw frightening parallels between injustice and racism in South Africa, and in Nazi Germany.

At that time he was elected as acting Moderator of the

Transvaal Synod. Beyers believed that this was 'the hand of God guiding me into a new direction', for the job involved travelling, and he met many people from African, coloured, and Indian congregations. So he saw the damaging results of the apartheid laws for himself. Then came Sharpville. On March 21st, 1960, a peaceful protest march was met with official violence. Sixty-nine were shot – most of them in their backs as they fled. Beyers Naudé did not lose his faith in God, and he continues to work as a Church leader. But he realised that in South Africa his Christian faith must involve him in politics – so he works energetically, but peacefully, for radical change.

2   *To ponder and discuss.* 'Those who say that religion has nothing to do with politics do not know what religion means' (Gandhi). 'Are not Religion and Politics the same Thing? Brotherhood is Religion' (William Blake). 'Let us say that the objective is the salvation of souls. Then everything must be arranged to achieve that end' quoted by John Lang, Dean of Lichfield, who continued, 'Even if that is too simple it is fundamentally right.' 'The Church is not there to preserve itself' (Roy Stevens). 'The Christian church is the one organisation in the world that exists purely for the benefit of non-members' (William Temple). 'When I give food to the poor they call me a saint. When I ask why the poor have no food, they call me a communist' (Archbishop Helder Camara). 'I find myself, unlike the contemporary Church, thinking more and more about the next world and less and less about the third world' (Alexander Dru).

Part 3

THE MYSTERY OF GOD

I fell at his feet as though dead.

St John the divine

I am not a God of far off, I am a brother and friend;

William Blake

God moves in a mysterious way
His wonders to perform;
He plants His footsteps in the sea,
And rides upon the storm.

Ye fearful saints, fresh courage take,
The clouds ye so much dread
Are big with mercy, and shall break
In blessings on your head.

William Cowper

I am fainthearted but in thee is help;
I am distressed – in thee is peace . . .
I do not understand thy ways,
But thou wilt know the way for me.

Dietrich Bonheffer
(written in the year of his martyrdom: 1943)

13

SILENT GOD

Charles Elliott, one-time director of Christian Aid, describes an incident in a refugee camp in El Salvador. People in the camp were talking about their faith, but one elderly man walked away and Charles Elliott followed him. As they talked, the elderly man asked a deep question: 'Why is God so silent?'

Last Christmas we received a letter from a young man who looked back over the year and described it as 'terrible'. His father had died – slowly and painfully – following a long illness. Our friend had prayed for him frequently. Apparently his prayers were not answered, and his question to us was the same as that of the elderly refugee. Many people prayed fervently for the recovery of David Watson, the highly-gifted rector of St Michael-le-Belfrey in York. In February 1984 he died of cancer in his early fifties. David was mourned by thousands.

A few years ago I visited the intensive-care ward of a hospital and sat by the bedside of a young woman. She was deeply unconscious following a car crash. The situation looked hopeless, and I sat with her parents as the consultant broke the news as gently as possible. When he had gone, the girl's mother turned to me and burst out in anger and anguish: 'I shall never call God Father again.' Well, that girl did recover and her mother did call God Father again. God was not silent on that occasion – but it looked for some time as though he was going to be.

The most famous example of a person wrestling with the silence of God is Job in the Old Testament. And the anguish which God's apparent inactivity can cause is summed up in the Psalmist's lament:

Why, O Lord, do you stand far off?
Why do you hide yourself in times of trouble?
(Ps. 10:1).

How long, O Lord?
Will you forget me for ever?
How long will you hide your face from me?
(Ps. 13:1).

How can we relate these not uncommon experiences of the silence of God to the teaching of Jesus on prayer – and to his insistence that we should approach God as our heavenly Father?

Jesus' teaching on prayer

Sometimes Jesus makes prayer sound very easy indeed. 'Ask and it will be given you' (Matt. 7:7). A simple prayer and the nearest mountain will obligingly skip into the ocean (Matt. 21:21). Some people make this a crucial test of the validity of the Christian faith. Mark Twain's street-wise character, Huckleberry Finn, patiently explained why he gave up praying.

Miss Watson she took me in the closet and prayed, but nothing come of it. She told me to pray every day, and whatever I asked for I would get it. But it warn't so. I tried it. Once I got a fish-line, but no hooks. It warn't any good to me without hooks. I tried for the hooks three or four times, but somehow I couldn't make it work . . .

I set down, one time, back in the woods, and had a long think about it. I says to myself, if a body can get anything they pray for, why don't Deacon Winn get back the money he lost on pork? Why can't the widow get back her silver snuffbox that was stole? Why can't Miss Watson fat up? No, says I to myself, there ain't nothing in it.

He asked for what he wanted. He didn't get it. *Conclusion:* it doesn't work, so why bother? Clearly, this is not a valid test of prayer. But it does ring some bells in our puzzled minds. On the one hand – extravagant promises. On the other hand – many of our most urgent prayers appear to go unanswered. At best it all seems hit or miss; at worst it doesn't seem to work at all.

I was reminded of this in a recent conversation. Last summer Rose made three requests. First, she prayed for a job; then she prayed for suitable accommodation; finally she prayed for a husband. (Not just any old husband; she had one particular young man in mind!) Her first two requests were met in full. The third request (by far the most important for Rose) appeared not to penetrate the ceiling. Why? Well, I could not give her a satisfactory answer, but as we talked four points emerged.

1 *Persevere.* Despite those amazing promises about mountains hopping into the sea, Jesus did not pretend that prayer would always bring instant results. He told a parable about a woman who kept on asking a judge ('pestering' is a more accurate word) for justice to be done. Jesus used this to teach an important lesson on prayer. *Persevere.* Don't give up. Our prayers are sometimes answered with: 'Yes, but not yet. Learn patience. Wait.'

However concerned we are with the answers to our prayers, God is concerned *with us as people.* He takes every opportunity to strengthen our faith which, like muscle, grows with exercise. If everything simply fell into our laps we should become very flabby, spiritually. God's way is more bracing: '. . . we know that suffering produces perseverance; perseverance, character; and character, hope. And hope does not disappoint us, because God has poured out his love into our hearts' (Rom. 5:3–5). I suspect that God sometimes remains silent because he wants to reduce *us* to silence. In his presence we must learn to listen as well as to speak.

2   *Prayer is not magic.* Faith is not a magic wand; God is not a genie in a lamp. If God is to answer Rose's urgent prayer that Tim will ask her to marry him, then he will need to change Tim's attitude towards Rose. Let us suppose that Tim is in fact in love with Mary, and that he is planning to ask Mary to marry him. Let us further suppose that Tim is also praying very devoutly that Mary will say, 'I will'. It is logically impossible for God to answer both prayers with a 'Yes'.

We begin to see the complications! Not that God is defeated by complexity. We know that '. . . in all things God works for the good of those who love him' (Rom. 8:28). This is a deeply-held Christian conviction. But, much as I dislike the thought, it is very clear that prayer is not a simple and automatic means of ensuring that I get my own way.

3   *Christians pray in the name of Jesus.* By this we understand that prayer is not a question of persuading God to change his mind, and to do our bidding. Often, it is a question of allowing God to bring *our* wills into line with *his*. Of course, God's will may be a very pleasant thing; medicine does not *have* to taste nasty in order to do us good. I believe it is my Christian duty to visit an elderly man with failing eyesight. Duty and pleasure are entirely at one in this matter, for I greatly enjoy the lively conversation – and the cream-cakes!

But on occasions, attempting to pray and to act 'in the name of Jesus' can be painful and difficult – for it does often involve me in a change of attitude. For example, it will certainly mean abandoning any pleasure which planning revenge might bring. Experienced Christians tell us that prayer gradually brings far-reaching changes of outlook into our lives. Then God can indeed give us the desires of our hearts as he longs to do (Ps. 37:4), for they become holy desires.

One further point: praying in the name of Jesus does not mean that our requests must be limited to 'the spiritual realm'. Many prayers in the New Testament are for spiritual qualities – like an increase in love, faith and wisdom. But the Lord's Prayer makes it crystal clear that we should pray for daily bread as well as for daily forgiveness. Alas, praying for daily bread is quite different from praying for daily cake.

4 *'No' is an answer, too.* This follows naturally from the description of God as Abba Father. I recall one of our daughters trying to reach a sharp knife on the kitchen table. She wanted it badly, but she was very young and knives are dangerous. On occasions, good parents acting out of love say 'wait' or 'no' to their children's requests.

There are two celebrated examples of prayers answered with a firm 'No' in the New Testament. The first is found on the lips of Jesus. In the Garden of Gethsemane he prayed: 'Father, everything is possible for you. Take this cup from me. Yet not what I will, but what you will' (Mark 14:36). That prayer *was* answered – with the most significant refusal in all history.

The second example is found in the letters of St Paul. He had what he terms, 'a thorn in my flesh'. We don't know what this refers to – some writers have suggested that it was epilepsy, or depression, or an eye complaint. However, we do know the answer to his prayers. Three times he asked; three times he received a firm 'No'. St Paul learnt deep lessons through this disappointing refusal – in particular he discovered that God's strength is made perfect in weakness (2 Cor. 12:9).

Promises. In the next chapter we shall look at the positive side of this problem, and I shall give several examples of occasions when God has appeared to answer and to act. But before moving to that area, let us imagine a woman who has never enjoyed a remarkable and obvious answer to her petitions. Despite this, she continues to be faithful in prayer and regular in worship. Would such a person need to speak of the silence of God?

To this question I would give an emphatic 'No'; for God is never completely silent. He *has* spoken. In the Bible he has given glorious promises. Throughout history he has provided many witnesses to his love: prophets, saints, martyrs – and many disciples who, though not famous, ring true. Most important of all, he has sent his Son. The writer of the letter to the Hebrews put it like this: 'In the past God spoke to our forefathers through the prophets at many times and in various ways. But in these last days he has spoken to us by his Son' (Heb. 1:1–2). St John puts this truth even more eloquently. In his famous prologue (John 1:1–18) he refers to Jesus as the very Word who came from God – stressing that he is the supreme means by which God speaks to his world.

Even in our darkest moments, when God seems distant (or even absent), he is far from being silent. He *always* speaks to us in his Son, who also experienced the deep darkness of the apparent absence of his heavenly Father, when he needed him most. So he cried from the cross using the Psalmist's words: 'My God, my God, why have you forsaken me?' (Ps. 22:1 and Mark 15:34). We, like him, are called to walk by faith and not by sight (2 Cor. 5:7). The proof of the pudding is in the promises. And the promises are as reliable as the Promiser himself.

POSTSCRIPT

1   The Father uttered one Word.
    That Word was his Son, and he utters him in
        everlasting silence;
    and in silence the soul has to hear it.

St John of the Cross

2   *Alec Guinness and the young boy*. In his autobiography (*Blessings in Disguise*, Fontana, 1986) Alec Guinness describes how he gradually moved from hostility towards, to membership of, the Roman Catholic Church. A whole

complex of events led up to this, including one brief
encounter with an unknown boy through which we might
say that God 'spoke' to the actor. He was filming *Father
Brown* in France and at dusk he walked back to his hotel,
dressed as a Catholic priest. Suddenly a boy of seven or
eight appeared, clutched his hand and walked with him.
Alec Guinness comments:

> He was full of excitement, hops, skips and jumps, but
> never let go of me. Although I was a total stranger he
> obviously took me for a priest and so to be trusted . . . I
> was left with an odd calm sense of elation. Continuing my
> walk I reflected that a Church which could inspire such
> confidence in a child, making its priests, even when
> unknown, so easily approachable could not be as schem-
> ing and creepy as so often made out. I began to shake off
> my long-taught, long-absorbed prejudices.

3   *Living by Faith.* I recall a conversation with a man whose
faith in God had been shaken in his teenage years, when
he realised that Christianity could not provide answers to
all of his questions. Now a mature Christian, he realises
that God is very *practical*. He gives us enough light to live
by, but does not always satisfy our curiosity, nor remove
our bewilderment – especially about suffering.

Faith involves living with some hard questions which we
cannot answer, in the light of the great answers which we *do*
possess. This is not *blind* faith, for God's clearest answer to
our greatest questions – questions concerning life, death
and the love of God – is found in Jesus Christ.

14

GOD WHO ANSWERS AND ACTS

In the previous chapter we considered the apparent silence of God, and the puzzle of prayers which do not appear to be heard or answered. This is a deep problem, and those who believe in God are bound to acknowledge that he does sometimes deal with us in an austere manner. Now we look at the other side of that particular coin. To this end, I shall give some examples of the way in which God appears to have answered, acted or spoken.

I have used the word 'appears', because in the nature of things we can never be certain. It is always open to the unbeliever to assert that these things would have happened anyway. On this view, the fact that we prayed at the 'right' time is simply a coincidence. So be it. If God chooses to leave open that particular door of interpretation, I shall not attempt to close it. Instead I shall offer a few examples for consideration, along with a reminder of Archbishop William Temple's assertion (a wise or foolish dictum, depending on your viewpoint) that when he stopped praying, coincidences stopped happening.

1   *An unexpected gift.* St Paul's church in York (of which I am a member) launched a special fund to pay for much-needed work on the interior of the church building. Half the money raised was to be given to our sister church in inner-city Bradford. One Sunday a final appeal was made, prayers were offered and gifts were pledged. The next day we received a letter announcing a large gift (£12,000) from a local Trust Fund. Not only had we more or less forgotten that we had applied to that Trust, but on that very day our parish was on the diocesan prayer diary – which means that people from all over Yorkshire were praying for us.

It is easy to dismiss this as mere coincidence – and I

concede that it may be nothing more than that. But viewed as part of a wider pattern – one experience among many others – the believer is prepared to recognise the hand of God. An outrageously biased viewpoint, or the logical outcome of faith and prayer. Which of these interpretations is accepted depends not on the event itself – but on a multitude of prior events, and on the view of the world adopted *before* the incident happened.

2 *Grandma saves the day.* A Welsh woman was talking about her childhood. She told me that her baby brother became seriously ill, and although he received medical treatment at home, he got no better. His grandmother wrapped the baby up, took him in her arms and stood in the road – praying that God would do something. Ten minutes later an ambulance drove down the road. Grandma flagged the vehicle down and the baby was taken to hospital, where he recovered.

3 *Your radio must go.* A woman was saving up for a radio. When she got the money together, she had a dream in which God appeared to tell her to give it all away. She was annoyed, but she could not get the thought out of her mind, so she did as she was 'told'. A few days later someone who knew nothing about her savings or her giving, presented her with a better radio than she had intended to purchase.

4 *A haircut and a healing.* Some readers will recognise the situation which I have just described. For a persistent '. . . do this . . . do this . . . do this . . .' is not uncommon. In an essay entitled 'The Efficacy of Prayer' (*Fernseed and Elephants*, Collins, 1975), C. S. Lewis describes how he experienced a nagging 'voice' in his mind, telling him to get his hair cut. Eventually he gave in. When he arrived, his barber said, 'Oh, I was praying you might come today.' Had Lewis delayed his visit, he would have been unable to help. He comments: 'It awed me; it awes me still. But of course one cannot rigorously prove a causal connection between the barber's prayers and my visit. It might be telepathy. It might be accident.'

He goes on to relate an incident concerning his wife Joy.

I have stood by the bedside of a woman whose thigh-bone was eaten through with cancer and who had thriving colonies of the disease in many other bones as well. It took three people to move her in bed. The doctors predicted a few months of life: the nurses (who often know better), a few weeks. A good man laid his hands on her and prayed. A year later the patient was walking (uphill, too, through rough woodland) and the man who took the last X-ray photos was saying, 'These bones are as solid as rock. It's miraculous.' But once again there is no rigorous proof. Medicine, as all true doctors admit, is not an exact science . . .

I am aware that 'giving in' too often to the voice in our heads can be dangerous for some people. For it might lead to a neurotic compulsion. And I admit that I have never had an experience exactly like that. But from time to time I see a clear picture in my mind of a friend, or of someone I have met only once or twice. When this happens, I conclude that God is prompting me to pray for that person, and I do so there and then – whether I am walking down the street, or driving, or writing, or whatever else.

5 *From the labour camps*. One remarkable and recent example of God apparently speaking and acting in answer to prayer, has been recounted by Irina Ratushinskaya. Irina spent four years in Soviet prisons and labour camps for her literary and human-rights activities. Just before Christmas 1986, she was released.

Christians in the West sometimes feel very inadequate alongside their Soviet brothers and sisters: life for us seems so very comfortable. But Irina does not see it like that. It is a question of working out our discipleship where God places us, for it is not our 'fault' if our situation is relatively easy. Indeed, she makes it clear that Soviet Christians could not survive without us. They need our interest and prayers, just as we need their courage and inspiration. She expresses this in one of her prison poems, from which I extract two verses:

Believe me, it was often thus
In solitary cells, on winter nights
A sudden sense of joy and warmth
And a resounding note of love

And then, unsleeping; I would know
A huddle by an icy wall
Someone is thinking of me now
Petitioning the Lord for me.

Irina's description of herself as 'a huddle by an icy wall'
gives a harrowing picture of the biting cold, the inadequate
clothing and the poor diet. But she testifies to two kinds of
warmth which she sometimes experienced – the inner
emotional warmth of joy, and a physical warmth throughout her body despite the freezing conditions. It is her
conviction that these phenomena (experienced by other
prisoners, too) were a direct answer to prayer. 'A sudden
sense of joy and warmth . . . someone is thinking of me
now – petitioning the Lord for me.'

She cannot *prove* that these things were answers to
prayer, but we cannot doubt that they happened, for she is
a woman of deep integrity and honesty. So I would gently
press the question: what other explanation fits?

6   *George Muller and the Bristol orphans*. During the last
century there were many unwanted and homeless children
in Britain's cities. It was an era when children's homes
flourished. Best known and largest is a chain of homes (now
stretching around the world) started by Thomas John
Barnado.

At about the same time, another Christian called George
Muller founded a home in Bristol. He believed that God
was calling him to do two things. First, to found a home for
children in need. Second, to prove the power of prayer. So
George refused to ask for money, food or clothing. If
he and his helpers, or the children in their care, needed
anything, he would resort to one strategy and one strategy
only – he would pray. He kept a remarkable diary which
reveals that his home was often down to its last coin or loaf
of bread. But the children never went hungry or unclothed.
Something, or someone, always turned up.

7   *The day I saved the world*. (Well . . . perhaps!) It was
just before Christmas, and I was sitting in the dining-hall in
the college where I worked, when the bursar asked for my
help. He had with him a rather distressed visitor – a patient
from our local psychiatric hospital. She told me (with great
urgency) that she had 'received' information about a great
catastrophe, which was about to engulf the world. I
suggested that there was only one solution to the problem:
we must pray. She readily agreed, so we went into the
college chapel and I prayed for her and for the world. She
left in a calmer state of mind, and no disaster struck. I live
to tell the tale, and you live to read it!

Now I do not see myself as a saviour of the world,
although I am a little reluctant to write off the insights of
that distressed woman as crazy nonsense. Her 'revelation'
may have been nothing more than a delusion, of course.
Delusion or not, I continue to believe that prayer achieves
more – much more – than we often realise.

This was certainly the view of Thomas Merton, one of the
great spiritual writers of our century. In 1941 he visited an
American monastery called Gethsemani, shortly before
joining the community. It was a dark and troubled time in
world history, especially in Europe where the Nazis were
causing havoc. As he watched the Trappist monks at
prayer, he came to see that activity as a focus of spiritual
power. He wrote this in his *Secular Journal*:

> This is the center of America. I had wondered what was
> keeping the country together, what has been keeping the
> universe from cracking in pieces and falling apart. It is
> places like this monastery – not only this one: there must
> be others . . . This is the only real city in America – and it
> is by itself, in the wilderness. It is an axle around which
> the whole country blindly turns, and knows nothing
> about it. Gethsemani holds the country together . . .
> 'What *right* have I to be here?'

In his view it was prayer – that mysterious and powerful
means by which human beings are caught up in the plans
and purposes of God – which holds the universe together
and checks chaos. Archbishop Michael Ramsey made the

same point. He asserted that worship brings healing into a broken world, because it is a channel through which the love of God flows into our lives. Fanciful? Perhaps; but perhaps not. Those who believe in God will find such insights bold but inspiring. Those who are less sure about God, will inevitably be less sure about the significance which these writers attribute to prayer.

8   *Learn the language*. On Sunday, November 22nd, 1987, the Barinov family arrived in Britain. Their arrival was attended by television cameras and great publicity – another dissident released from the Soviet Union. Valeri Barinov is a rock singer and Christian evangelist who spent time in Soviet labour camps. Two days after his arrival in Britain I shook him by the hand – much to my surprise.

Michael Bourdeaux, with whom the Barinov family were staying, had been booked a year earlier to speak at a conference which I was attending. He brought Valeri with him, who spoke to his first English audience that Tuesday evening. His ability to do this resulted from a message 'given' (by God, she claimed) to a Russian friend of the Barinovs a few years earlier. 'When are you going to learn English, Valeri?' she asked. 'Never!' he replied. But she insisted that God wanted him to – and he yielded. His English is good, but for one glorious moment he forgot himself and burst into enthusiastic Russian! I wondered if I would be prepared to tackle the hard work of learning Russian on the basis of another person's faith.

Mention of Michael Bourdeaux reminds me of one of the most remarkable answers to prayer of which I know. Michael works ceaselessly on behalf of religious believers of all faiths in Communist lands. He started this work as a result of a 'coincidence' which brought people together from distant countries at precisely the right time. I won't describe this at length because I summarised it in my previous book. Michael Bourdeaux gives his own account in *Risen Indeed: Lessons in Faith from the USSR*. (For details see the note at the end of this chapter.)

9   *From tramp to social worker*. While writing this chapter I received through the post a leaflet seeking support for the

fine work among homeless men, based at St George's Church in Leeds. The leaflet includes poignant accounts of men who eat the food and use the beds, but whose life style is unaffected and unaltered. Among all this realism the following examples stand out. I print them without comment.

For twenty years Ron lived in psychiatric care. When he came to us he was utterly lost and bewildered. At the least frustration he would go to pieces – smashing windows – tearing up money – gashing his arms. As a result he was barred from hostels and remained an outcast. In spite of all this, Ron had a simple faith in God. He would ask us to pray with him. Somewhere he had learned by heart some simple prayers. He would pray for us in his own words as we cared for him. Wonderfully his prayers were answered: now, a few years on, he has a home of his own among ordinary people in an ordinary street in Leeds. He keeps it spotless.

We could give countless stories of men and women from throughout Britain who, like Ron, have learned to settle down. One man, for years a wandering hopeless alcoholic, has stopped drinking, married, got a degree and qualified as a social worker!

10 *A book on the subject.* Rex Gardner is an experienced doctor – a Fellow of the Royal College of Obstetricians and Gynaecologists. In a carefully researched book entitled, *Healing Miracles: A Doctor Investigates* (DLT, 1987), he examines several reports of miracles. I will pull out one example, almost at random.

In 1976 four Christians (one Nepalese, three missionaries), travelled to a remote area of Nepal to start a leprosy clinic. One of the missionaries fell on to a metal pipe and ruptured his spleen. Another missionary – a doctor – gave him morphine and set up a saline intravenous infusion. They had no surgical equipment and an urgent message requesting help was not delivered. After two hours – at the request of the injured man – the three others gathered round him, read a Bible passage about healing (Jas. 5:14–15), prayed and anointed him with oil. His pulse and blood pressure rapidly improved, and he recovered. News of this spread, and the incident was a great help in establishing the leprosy project. Rex Gardner, and the missionary doctor involved in the incident, believe that the recovery was in answer to prayer.

11   *An unremarkable answer.* We sometimes picture St Paul as a prime example of self-sufficient man – travelling huge distances with great confidence and panache. In fact, as we study his letters we see that he experienced fear and depression, and badly needed the support and love of friends. In his second letter to the Corinthian Church he writes about 'the Father of compassion and the God of all comfort' (2 Cor. 1:3). Later, he admits that when he and Timothy arrived in Macedonia, they were plagued with 'conflicts on the outside and fears within'. He goes on to say that God heard their prayers: '. . . but God, who comforts the downcast, comforted us . . .'

Now during his lifetime Paul received a whole series of remarkable spiritual experiences. God spoke to him in dreams and visions, and he was filled with God's Spirit. So we might wonder how God would answer Paul's prayer for comfort and help – and expect something dramatic.

In fact, his prayers for help were answered in a very *un*remarkable manner. The verse quoted above ends like this, 'But God, who comforts the downcast, comforted us by the coming of Titus' (2 Cor. 7:6). It is a lovely anti-climax. Not an angel; not a vision; not a dream; *but a friend*. I suspect that God often answers our prayers in the ordinary events of daily life. I further suspect that we in-adequate, sinful human beings are quite often the answer to other people's prayers – when we make a particular visit to a particular person at just the 'right' time, for example.

12   *A mysterious answer* (or no answer at all?). During the last century, a British naval officer believed that he was called by God to establish missionary work in Tierra del Fuego – that very inhospitable area at the southern tip of South America. No doubt the work began in prayer, and continued in prayer. Yet disaster struck. The ship carrying

provisions failed to arrive, and during the winter of 1850 the whole party died of starvation.

When their bodies were discovered, the following paragraph was found in Allen Gardiner's diary: 'Poor and weak as we are, our boat is a very Bethel of our souls, for we feel and know that God is here. Asleep or awake, I am, beyond the power of expression, happy.'

Despite this tragic setback, others continued the work and Allen Gardiner's vision was fulfilled. In 1872 the first Tierra del Fuegans were baptised. Charles Darwin registered his surprise and admiration at the work of the missionaries, and expressed his delight at being elected an honorary member of the South American Missionary Society (which continues to do excellent work today).

Conclusion. I refrained from ending on a triumphant note, because an ambiguous and disappointing example is characteristic of much of the evidence for the God who answers and acts. Prayer includes great mysteries, and the apparent silence of God on some occasions is only one of these. To me there is an even greater mystery. Why does God encourage us to pray at all? It seems that he always chooses to involve us in his activities whenever possible, rather than 'go it alone'. But *why* he should do so is beyond my understanding, although the following illustration might help us to glimpse one possible reason.

I know a school chaplain who involves his students as fully as possible in chapel services. Sometimes this makes worship rather ragged. A nervous child might mumble the prayers; a hesitant child might stumble over the reading. The services would be much more polished if my friend chose to lead them himself – for he has an excellent voice and considerable 'presence'. But he has no intention of changing his policy. Involving the children is good for them, good for the other worshippers and good for him. He gets much more satisfaction from an unpolished team effort, than from an impeccable solo performance.

Perhaps there is a parallel here with the way in which God relates to us. But it is only a hint and, alas, complete answers to our questions are not on offer. Much ink and effort have been used in an attempt to cast light on the mystery of prayer. Yet when all has been said, Christians continue to pray, mainly because Jesus told them to. As disciples we follow our Master. This is not blind faith nor unthinking obedience. We gladly follow him because we are convinced that he speaks with unrivalled authority. So even when his teaching appears to lead us into a maze, we still follow with confidence.

We could be mistaken, of course. Our reasons for praying are only as good as our reasons for acknowledging him as Son of God, and Lord of Life. If we are right, then we should be extremely foolish *not* to accept his teaching on prayer – or on anything else. This book is not the place to outline the reasons for my steadily deepening conviction that this is in fact the case. Instead, I will end this chapter with a point which has often been made, but which bears repetition. It is much harder than is commonly supposed to give a satisfactory explanation for all that Jesus said and did, and for everything that resulted from his coming. Unless we resort to New Testament terminology and Christian concepts, that is. And if we do *that*, we are in for the complete package deal – prayer included.

POSTSCRIPT

On page 106 I quoted the Psalmist who lamented the silence of God. At the end of this chapter it will be appropriate to return to the same Psalm. Having wrestled with his problem the Psalmist asserts,

> But I trust in Your unfailing love;
> my heart rejoices in your salvation,
> I will sing to the Lord,
> for He has been good to me.
> (Ps. 13:5–6).

Note (see page 117). *Risen Indeed*, Michael Bourdeaux (DLT, 1983). My summary of Michael's remarkable coincidence can be found in *The Case Against Christ* (pp. 188–9). In that book I also outline my reasons for believing in Jesus as the Son of God and risen Lord.

15

COMPLEX GOD

> But the Godhead of the Father, of the Son, and of the Holy Ghost, is all one: the Glory equal, the Majesty co-eternal.
> Such as the Father is, such is the Son: and such is the Holy Ghost.
> The Father uncreate, the Son uncreate: and the Holy Ghost uncreate.
> The Father incomprehensible, the Son incomprehensible: and the Holy Ghost incomprehensible.
> The Father eternal, the Son eternal: and the Holy Ghost eternal.
> And yet they are not three eternals: but one eternal.
> As also there are not three incomprehensibles, nor three uncreated: but one uncreated, and one incomprehensible (From the *Creed of St Athanasius*).

And so we could go on . . . That creed – however profound it might be – is beyond most of us. It feels dusty; it belongs to another age. If we share the same truths, we don't express them in the same way.

But even if we use modern language, we don't altogether remove the problem. For Christians still appear to be bad at mathematics. We still speak about the Trinity, and we cannot escape the fact that while 'Three in One and One in Three' may be good theology, it is very bad arithmetic – and rather difficult to grasp. Which accounts for the advice given by older clergy to their curates: 'Always get a visiting preacher on Trinity Sunday!'

However, I am convinced that this insistence on God as Trinity is vitally important. I also believe that the problem is not unique – nor quite as complicated as it seems at first sight.

1 Parallels from science

Deep truths are by definition . . . well, deep! When we get to the boundaries of our understanding, we cannot avoid stretching language to its limits. Certainly this is true within science.

I recall watching a television programme on astronomy. An expert was talking about our 'finite but expanding universe'. The interviewer looked puzzled and asked: 'If the universe is finite, then it has limits. So . . . if I get to the edge, will I fall off?' The astronomer laughed. 'If you understood the concepts involved, you would see that the question you are asking is, quite literally – nonsense.' Clearly such concepts are mighty difficult to grasp – and mighty hard to communicate, too. Ordinary language cannot cope.

To take another example: the nature of light puzzled scientists for many years. The problem was that in some situations light behaved like a series of waves, while in other situations it behaved like a stream of particles. It couldn't be both, but . . . One scientist mischievously said that he thought of light as waves on Mondays, Wednesdays and Fridays, and as particles on the other days of the week. (No doubt he was grateful for Sunday, when he could exercise his mind on easier concepts – like the Trinity!)

Paul Dirac saved the day when in 1928 he put forward an explanation, and framed a theory, which accounts for all the conflicting evidence. In the same way, the doctrine of the Trinity is an attempt by Christians to give a coherent explanation for the various experiences which point them to God.

In the eighteenth century, Samuel Johnson wanted to make a point about the permanence and reliability of the physical world. So he kicked a stone. Today, scientists would question his 'proof'. 'Look closer' and you will find that a stone is made up mostly of empty space, containing zooming packets of energy. What is more, while it is possible to know the position or speed of these particles, it is not possible to know both at once.

Scientists who investigate subatomic particles are well used to dealing with difficult concepts which stretch their language and their imaginations. So they draw pictures, and make models, and speak in metaphors. But they are keen to point out that we cannot pin reality down. The pictures are no more than useful approximations to reality itself.

This is helpful background when we talk about God. We have the very highest authority for speaking about him in picture language. Father, judge, and king, are three descriptions which Jesus used. But we shall never pin God down. We talk in approximations – some of which are useful; some of which can be misleading. We need to express these insights in language appropriate to our culture. But we shall be unwise to discard the wisdom of men and women of earlier generations altogether. For many of them were holier than we are, and some were companions of the Ultimate Expression of God's nature: Jesus Christ himself.

2   All good doctrine is rooted in experience

The doctrine of the Trinity was not dreamed up by scholars thinking deep thoughts in quiet libraries. This formula was the only way in which the early Christians could make sense of their experiences of God – and what amazing experiences they were!

The first disciples were Jews – devout monotheists who frequently recited the Shema: 'The Lord our God, the Lord is one' (Deut. 6:4). Then they met Jesus. At no point did they abandon their belief in the One God. It would have been unthinkable for them to become bi-theists (believers in two Gods). Yet their concept of God was greatly enlarged as a result of their contact with Jesus. So, while continuing to assert that God is *One*, they began to speak of God the Father, and of God the Son. Indeed, it is clear that within a short period of time they had firmly placed Jesus, the man from Nazareth, on the *Godward* side of that line which divides humanity from divinity.

For example, in St Paul's letter to the Philippians, we find a lovely hymn to Christ. It is likely that Paul was quoting words already well known to the early Christian communities. Whether Paul or another poet wrote it, it is clear that the hymn is modelled on a passage from the Old

Testament, which is strongly monotheistic in tone. I will set out a few verses side by side for easy comparison.

At the name of Jesus every knee should bow in heaven and on earth and under the earth, and every tongue confess that Jesus Christ is Lord, to the glory of God the Father. (Phil. 2:10–11).	Turn to me and be saved, all you ends of the earth; for I am God, and there is no other . . . Before me every knee will bow; by me every tongue will swear. (Isa. 45:22–3).

From this and other passages we are left in no doubt that when the early Christians called Jesus 'Lord', they were not politely addressing him as 'Sir'.[1] No. They were thinking of the Jewish Scriptures. Indeed, they were applying to Jesus the name used for *God* in the Greek translation of the Hebrew Bible (our Old Testament).

This would present no problems if they had been Romans, not Jews. For Romans believed in many gods, and were quite used to including men (like the emperors) in their pantheon of gods. But the Jews set their face against this. They reacted so strongly against it that they made a thorough nuisance of themselves throughout the Roman Empire. Indeed, so strong was their belief in monotheism, that many of them were prepared to die rather than compromise. *One God only*

So it is shocking and startling to find these Christian Jews placing the *man* Jesus on the *Godward* side of reality – as surprising as it would be to find a group of Muslims today speaking of Muhammad as divine. They *never* do that. Allah alone is God, and Muhammad is his prophet. A very special man, yes. But a human being, and nothing more nor other than a human being. So the line between God and humanity is firmly drawn by Muslims – with Muhammad clearly on the human side.

---

[1] Professor James Dunn amplifies this in *The Evidence for Jesus* (SCM, 1985). Professor C. F. D. Moule suggests that the early Christian phrase 'in Christ' points to the same conclusion (*The Phenomenon of the New Testament*, SCM, 1967).

The Jews were – and are – just as tenacious in their belief in the one God as Muslims are. Yet this small, but growing, group of Jews appeared to break ranks, by calling Jesus 'Lord'. It caused them endless trouble, yet they denied that they had joined the Romans by becoming polytheists. To their hearers they were talking in riddles. We still believe in one God; and Jesus is divine too!

Now, of course, they could have been wrong. That is not the point. The question is: How can this amazing shift in attitude be explained? How can we account for the fact that these Jewish men and women (some of whom knew Jesus of Nazareth personally, and all of whom knew that he was a man who sweated and wept), could nevertheless address him as Lord (= God)? And how can we account for the fact that they did so consistently, and with such conviction, that they convinced more and more people?

I believe that there are three converging explanations for this great puzzle. First, they found the raw materials for this concept in the teaching of Jesus himself. Second, they found echoes of his teaching in their own Scriptures. Third, God raised Jesus from the dead. It took something as big as that to account for their amazing change in outlook. Because of his resurrection, they came to see that terms reserved for the very great were not adequate to describe Jesus. Even exalted words like prophet and Messiah did not quite capture his majesty.

No: puzzling as it was to them as well as to their hearers, they were forced to call Jesus . . . *Lord*. It was not deep philosophical analysis which led them to this conclusion; it was reflection upon their puzzling and startling experiences. How *could* they explain all that had happened to them as a result of meeting Jesus, and being with him, and listening to him? And how could they explain the empty tomb of Jesus? Above all, how could they explain the fact that Jesus had appeared to so many of them after his crucifixion?

Only by accepting that Jesus had been raised from the dead. And if he was lord over death he was, quite simply . . . LORD.

COMPLEX GOD: CONTINUED

To recap. Those early Jewish Christians believed that God is one. Unlike the Romans they were not polytheists; they did not believe in several gods. But their understanding of the one God was greatly enriched and enlarged, for they came to believe that Jesus was also divine. But Jesus was not the same as the Father. So . . . there were *two* Persons in their *one* God. They spoke about the Father and the Son.

But that wasn't the end of the matter. They were forced to understand and interpret another great experience, too. The early Christians knew about the Holy Spirit from their Jewish Scriptures. They knew that in the course of history, God sent his Spirit to particular people, to equip them for special service. They knew, too, that the prophet Jeremiah had predicted a new age, marked by a new covenant – and that the prophet Joel had looked forward to a day when God's Spirit would be 'poured out on all people'.

Then came the Jewish festival of Pentecost, six weeks after the first Easter Sunday. On that day they realised that God was with them (or rather within them) in a new and exciting way – giving them joy, courage and a deep sense of unity. They spoke of being filled with the Spirit of God. They did not doubt that it was God who was working in them, and they sometimes used phrases like 'the Holy Spirit', or 'the Spirit of Jesus'. But that presented a further puzzle. For God was also reigning in heaven, and Jesus was enthroned at his right hand.

So they came to think not of three gods, but of three persons in one God: Father, Son and Holy Spirit.

The New Testament writers did not attempt to tidy up these descriptions into a neat formula. They simply described their experiences and recorded their conclusions. But the beginnings of tidiness are evident. See, for example, St Paul's famous prayer: 'May the grace of the Lord Jesus Christ, and the love of God, and the fellowship of the Holy Spirit be with you all' (2 Cor. 13:14).

Christians who came after the New Testament period felt the need to get their thoughts in order – especially when faced with attacks upon their faith, by people who wanted to downgrade the importance of Jesus or the Holy Spirit.

As a result of drawing out the implications found within the New Testament – which was based upon the experiences of those first Christians – a phrase was coined. 'The doctrine of the Trinity; three persons in one God.'

In time, fuller statements of what this doctrine does and does not mean were hammered out. It was a kind of Christian equivalent to Paul Dirac's explanation for the apparently contradictory nature of light. For it fitted all the facts: the oneness of God and the richness of their experience. And it fits the experience of Christians today, too.

Practical implications
The implications of the doctrine of the Trinity are immense. I shall sketch three areas.

(a) *God is great and God is near.* Theologians talk about the 'transcendence' and the 'immanence' of God. Which simply means that God is *over* us, and that God is *with* us.

A divine clockmaker who started the world, then left it to unwind on its own: such a god inhabits many imaginations. But he does not inhabit eternity. This is not the Christian God. No: the God of the Bible did not light the blue touch-paper in the grand firework of creation, only to retire a great distance, with no further involvement and little further interest. The Scriptures speak of the great Creator God, who fashioned the heavens and the earth *ex nihilo* – out of nothing – and who *continues* to sustain everything by his love and power.

To recognise God as the majestic Creator is an important feature of Christian theology. From this it follows that we are stewards of his creation. Nature is not a gold-mine to be ransacked and exploited. It is to be respected, used and handed on in good order.

The Scriptures speak of the Holy God, majestic and awful (literally: to be approached with awe). All that Bible talk about thrones, and about Jesus sitting at the right hand of God, clearly points in that direction. He is King of Kings and Lord of Lords. But without the doctrine of the Trinity, we should be 'stuck' there – with a God so great that we

must approach him with reverence and awe, and *with an overwhelming sense of distance and separation*.

Instead, we are instructed to come with confidence – even with boldness – into his presence (Heb. 10:19–22). One of the loveliest titles given to Jesus – a name which we remember every Christmas – is Emmanuel, *God with us*. It is a powerful reminder that in Jesus, God came down to our level. As we ponder this fact, the command (given by Jesus himself) to 'fear God' is softened by a glimpse of why (and how) we should love God. For he has drawn very close. He comes to us as a little child; he walks with us as our human brother. *Our God has a human face as well as a heavenly throne.*

The wonderful truth about the Holy Spirit – the third person of the Trinity – underlines this for us. He draws near to us as the counsellor; he enters into us as the strengthener. So God is in heaven, and on earth at the same time. He is far above us. He is also closer than breathing. For he is Father, Son and Holy Spirit.

(b) *God does not need us*. In the Bible, the Church is described as the body of Christ. Because of this, some believers suggest that God needs us to do his work. 'He has no hands but our hands; no feet but our feet.' In a sense this is true. We are, in Bible language, 'fellow-workers with

God'. But only because – for our sakes – he has *chosen* to operate in this way. In his limitless power he has chosen to place limits on himself. It seems (for reasons which we must leave to him) that he prefers to work *with* us, and to enlist our co-operation whenever possible.

That is *his* decision. And he certainly does not need us for purposes of friendship and company! I recall attending an evangelistic meeting at which there was an 'altar call' or 'appeal'. The evangelist (a young man who was very effective in God's service: I do not criticise him harshly) gave the impression that we should be cheering up a rather lonely Jesus if we should 'decide for him'. Not so! The love which is generated between the three persons within the one godhead is perfect and complete. The Father, the Son and the Holy Spirit do not *need* John Jones and Betty Brown. But they do invite and welcome them. And us too, to our eternal enrichment.

(c) *God is for us*. One verse in St Paul's letter to the Romans means so much to me, that I asked for it to be printed on the order of service at our wedding, and Isabel readily agreed: 'He who did not spare his own Son, but gave him up for us all – how will he not also, along with him, graciously give us all things?' (8:32).

God is on our side. That is the meaning and the message of the doctrine of the Trinity. He loved us so much that he sent his Son for us. He continues to love us so much that he daily sends his Spirit into our hearts and lives. By this means, God strengthens and encourages us. He even prays within us.

Many Christians find prayer difficult. I often do, and then I recall this wonderful promise: 'We do not know what we ought to pray for, but the Spirit himself intercedes for us with groans that words cannot express' (Rom. 8:26). Equally encouraging is the fact that Jesus – risen, ascended and reigning with God the Father – prays *for* us. '. . . because Jesus lives for ever . . . he always lives to intercede' (Heb. 7:24–5; Rom. 8:34). Think of a day when you were lonely and miserable. No one cares about you; no one is praying for you. This is how you felt – *but you were wrong*. Whoever else might or might not be praying for you, *Jesus is*. You are in his prayers and enfolded in his love every moment of every day. What is more, he prays with deep understanding, for he too was tested and tempted as we are – although he did not sin.

Does this mean that God (the Son) prays to God (the Father)? Yes and no. For Jesus the Son of God continues through all eternity to be Jesus the one 'Proper Man'. The incarnation – by which God became man – is for all eternity, not just for thirty or so years. By this means he is Emmanuel – God with us. By the same means, the converse is true as well. He raises our humanity to heaven.

Yes, it *is* a mystery. And I don't pretend to be able to unravel it. But it is a *glorious* mystery, and I rejoice that it is rooted in history and in experience. I invite you to join me in praising God, for he is the blessed and divine Trinity: Father, Son and Holy Spirit. And I invite you to join me in thanking God that this great doctrine has so many practical implications for our daily lives.

POSTSCRIPT: ON RECEIVING THE HOLY SPIRIT

Over the past few years there has been a deepening awareness of the activity of God in people's lives, and much discussion of the role of the Holy Spirit. The Bible teaches that when we receive the Holy Spirit, God brings the *fruit* of the Spirit and the *gifts* of the Spirit into our lives.

1   *The fruit of the Spirit.* This concept is straightforward, and is based on two verses in the New Testament: '. . . the fruit of the Spirit is love, joy, peace, patience, kindness, goodness, faithfulness, gentleness and self-control' (Gal. 5:22–3). Two things are clear. First, all Christians should possess *all* of these qualities in some degree. Second, God gradually develops these qualities within us over the entire period of our lives. They do not come fully formed. Like fruit they grow gradually; like muscle they develop with exercise. So they are the litmus paper of Christian growth. *Question*: Am I making progress in the Christian life?

Answer: Am I more loving; is my faith a little stronger; do I have greater self-control than I had a year ago?

2 *The gifts of the Spirit*. In addition to bringing these lovely qualities into our lives, the Spirit bestows *gifts* as well. In various places in the New Testament, the gifts of the Spirit are listed. They range from love (so important that it is the only quality which is the fruit of the Spirit *and* a gift of the Spirit as well) to the abilities needed to be a good administrator within the Church.

Much attention has been focused on the more spectacular gifts, like speaking in tongues and healing. They are sometimes given the status of Christian litmus paper – the acid test of openness to God and mature Christian progress. Having given a great deal of thought to this question, I would gently dissent from this view. For unlike the fruit of the Spirit, the gifts of the Spirit are spread among the various members within the church. I have some gifts; you have other gifts. They are given, not for personal possession, but for the common good. As St Peter puts it: 'Each one should use whatever gift he has received to serve others' (1 Pet. 4:10).

So while we should be open to God and ready to receive all the gifts which he wishes to give us, we should not worry too much about this gift or that. Our faith is intended to *liberate* as well as to *challenge* us. Let's rejoice in what we've got; let's give thanks for gifts which others possess; let's be eager to receive those gifts which are yet to come (1 Cor. 14:1); and let's ensure that we are not neglecting to use the gifts we already have.

3 *Receiving the Spirit*. This, too, is a controversial subject. Some Christians would tie the coming of the Spirit to formal acts like baptism or confirmation. Others would apply a sacred formula – like prayer with laying on of hands – or urge people to attend a special service designed for this purpose. Each of these has a place, but we need to remember two points from the Gospels. First, St John emphasises that God's Spirit is sovereign. We cannot command him. 'The wind blows wherever it pleases' (John 3:8). Second, St Luke reminds us that while we cannot command him, we

can *invite* him. Here is the promise of Jesus: 'If you then, though you are evil, know how to give good gifts to your children, how much more will your Father in heaven give the Holy Spirit to those who ask him!' (Luke 11:13).

It is as easy as that. A simple prayer of invitation, and the Spirit will come into our lives. (Sometimes bringing a sense of great joy; sometimes coming more quietly. Jesus promises that he will come to us if invited – he does not specify *how*.) However simple, it is very far-reaching. For we are inviting the *Holy* Spirit. So we must be prepared for drastic changes in behaviour, attitude and outlook.

4   *The fullness of the Spirit.* Some Christians have further anxious questions. They have heard people talk about the 'fullness of the Spirit' and 'baptism in the Spirit' – and they wonder whether they are missing out on an extra dimension of spiritual experience.

Now there is a great deal which can be said about this – and I would recommend Michael Green's book *I Believe in the Holy Spirit* (Hodder, revised edition, 1985). For now, I will simply say that if this worries you, it probably means that you have no reason to worry! For phrases like the 'fullness of the Spirit' are applied in the New Testament to people who want to serve God with all their strength, and who know that they need God's renewing power if they are to do so. If you are worried about these questions, it almost certainly shows that you are in the correct frame of mind to invite the Spirit into your life. And Jesus has promised that he will come – not half-heartedly but abundantly!

One thing is crystal clear. The New Testament forbids us to think in terms of first-class Christians (those who have been baptised in the Spirit), and the also-rans. It is healthier – and happier – to think of ourselves as brothers and sisters in the family of God. Some may be more mature than others, but all have equal significance in God's eyes.

16

HE, SHE OR IT GOD?

At first I thought I had misheard. I was at a conference where most delegates referred to God in the usual way, with the pronouns He and Him.[1] A few used the word It – especially when referring to the Holy Spirit – and a small group of delegates consistently referred to God as She and Her.

It jarred. Indeed, it was rather like receiving a mental electric shock. Two questions rattled around within me. Did my reaction arise simply from the unfamiliarity of thinking of God as She, or was it more fundamental than that? To put it bluntly: are male terms appropriate, and female terms simply *in*appropriate, when we refer to God?

This led on to other questions. Is it right to think of God in personal terms at all? Perhaps we should be wiser to use impersonal, neutral terms like 'It'? These are important issues for our day and we shall get into deep water. So I shall marshal my thoughts under tidy headings, in an attempt to prevent the water from being murky as well as deep.

1   The case for thinking of God as He
(a) *Jesus: his personality*. 'No man has ever seen God: it is the only Son, who is nearest to the Father's heart, who has made him known' (John 1:18 JB) These famous words from the prologue to the Fourth Gospel take us to the heart of the Christian understanding of revelation. We finite human

---

[1] In common with most authors today, I usually write pronouns for God without capital letters. Not *He* but *he*. Most modern translators of the Bible do the same. But for the subject-matter of this chapter, it will be clearer to use the old convention when talking about God the Father. Hence *He* and *Him*, not *he* and *him*.

beings cannot sit down, think hard, and so work out what God is like. If accurate understanding is to take place, it must be on the basis of God's initiative.

Hence the importance of the Bible, for there we see men and women seeking to understand, and attend to, God. To put this another way: in the Bible we see God using the events in the world around them, to communicate with His people. As they seek to make sense of their lives, they begin to understand more about God, more of His faithfulness towards them, and more of His requirements from them.

Certain individuals stand out in this process. In particular, the great prophets were open to God. The Christian claim is that this long process came to a climax in Jesus – a thought which is beautifully expressed in the New Testament letter to the Hebrews: 'In the past God spoke to our forefathers through the prophets at many times and in various ways, but in these last days he has spoken to us by his Son' (Heb. 1:1–2).

The New Testament claims that Jesus reveals God to us in three ways. By who he is; by what he does; and by what he says. All three means of revelation indicate that it is appropriate to talk about God in human terms. For Jesus, who lived in Galilee and visited Jerusalem, was a human being – a male human being. Which suggests that it is appropriate to think of God as 'He'. Of course, this does not rule out the possibility that 'She' is all right, too.

(b) *Jesus: his teaching.* The major theme of Jesus' teaching was the Kingdom of God, and it is clear that the King in this Kingdom is God Himself. On other occasions Jesus likened God to a judge – and judges, like kings, were male. Most significant of all, he taught his hearers to think of God as their heavenly Father.

As we have seen, this picture has enormous implications as far as prayer and trust are concerned. It also has implications for the subject of this chapter. For if Jesus thought of God in personal terms – and in masculine terms at that – Christians cannot lightly set his teaching on one side. By its very nature, discipleship involves following our teacher

where he leads and points. We cannot follow him, and go
our own way at the same time.

2   The case for God as She

If we agree that Jesus' teaching about God as heavenly
Father is fundamental and cannot be put on one side, this
does not settle the matter. Perhaps we are at liberty to
supplement and enrich this teaching by referring to God as
our Mother, too? This was the point being made by those
women at the conference, and their argument was based on
two main grounds.

1.   The culture argument. This runs as follows: certain
customs and beliefs which we read about in the Bible have
lost their force for us. Few preachers today insist on women
keeping their heads covered in church, although we find
this teaching in the Bible. Such things were important *then*;
they are not important *now*. So we quietly set them on one
side.

Those women applied this argument to male emphases in
the Scriptures. The Bible was written in a male-dominated
society. Kings, not queens, ruled from Saul onwards, and
most judges and prophets were men. If these leadership
roles were filled by men, it is not surprising that God, the
supreme Leader, should be thought of in male terms in
ancient Israel.

But that is too simple, said those women – and they were
right! For one thing we find clear exceptions in the Bible.
Deborah was a leader in Israel (Judg. 4). Philip's four
daughters were prophetesses (Acts 21:9). In the New
Testament several leading church members were women.
Furthermore, two of the highest possible honours were
afforded to women. One Mary bore Jesus; another Mary
was the first to witness the empty tomb and to speak to the
risen Christ.

In any case, the world has moved on in its attitude to
women – and this is partly due to the teaching of the New
Testament. If you doubt this, look at some Islamic or
Hindu communities. In many of the former, women have
few rights or opportunities. In the latter, recent news

reports from the BBC establish that some widows continue to die illegally on their husbands' funeral fires, following the ancient Hindu custom of Suttee. In contrast to this, Jesus' attitude was bordering on the revolutionary and scandalous. A Jewish man talking alone with a fallen Samaritan woman was dynamite in his day.

St Paul – often dismissed as having a 'thing against women' – built on the teaching of Jesus. He was progressive for his time.[2] If the Western world has moved on in its attitude to women, this is partly due to the seeds sown in the Christian Scriptures. So – runs the argument – it is time for the Church to start catching up with the world.

2. *Direct teaching*. All this is important background, but it does not relate directly to the question of whether we might refer to God as She. We move to that now. For it is clear that certain strands within the Bible encourage us to think of God in feminine terms. For example, the Old Testament term 'Wisdom of God' refers to God Himself – and 'wisdom' is a feminine gender word in Hebrew and Greek. Similarly, 'dove' (used to represent the Holy Spirit) is a feminine word and symbol. In Genesis 1 we read that God made male *and female* 'in his image'. And in Isaiah we hear God's gentle encouragement: 'As a mother comforts her child, so I will comfort you.' (66:13)

Towards the end of his life Jesus often went to the Mount of Olives. On its slopes there is a garden called Gethsemane. At the foot of the hill runs the Kidron Valley, and on the other side stands the city of Jerusalem – lovely in the sunlight, and only a few minutes' walk from the hill with its olive trees. Jesus stood on that mount, looked across the valley and felt strong ties with the capital of his homeland. Then he crossed the valley and ascended to the city, where he taught. At one point he burst out: 'O Jerusalem, Jerusalem, you who kill the prophets and stone those sent to you, how often I have longed to gather your children

---

[2] Paul encouraged women to lead (e.g. Priscilla, Lydia and Phoebe) and to learn – unusual in the first century. For helpful discussion of these issues see *Men Women and God* (Ed. Kathy Keay, Marshall Pickering, 1987)

together, as a hen gathers her chicks under her wings, but you were not willing.' (Matt. 23:37).

It is a deeply moving moment – and a significant one. For to describe the depth of his love for his people, Jesus speaks tenderly and tearfully and uses a *feminine* picture. He explains that he often felt like a mother hen, longing to gather and protect her offspring.

So it is possible to build a case for thinking of God as She. But – if the Bible is to be our guide – there is no case for *replacing* He with She. For the Scriptures consistently use male terms for God, and prayers are offered to God as *He*. To insist on praying to God as She is to go down a road that can lead to pre-Christian paganism. I share Elaine Storkey's reservations. In *What's Right With Feminism* (SPCK, 1985), she writes: 'The argument is that for thousands of years before the rise of Judaism and Christianity and all the other "male" religions, the universal deity, the life-force of the universe, was the goddess.' She goes on to remind us that because a religion is old, it is not necessarily true.

3   The case for describing God as 'It'

Some people feel uneasy about using *any* kind of personal terms for God – whether male or female. Using personal images diminishes Him, they feel. We are all aware of the gibe that Christians think of God as a bearded old man sitting on a cloud. And we know that referring to Him as Father can lead to that. So it looks as though the critics have a point with some substance.

I once led a Bible study on the Psalms with a group of young people. We went through those poems in order to draw up a list of verbal pictures which are used to describe God. We stopped when we had gathered around thirty titles. As a result of our probe, we found that several of these are personal (and male): king, judge, shepherd . . . But several other titles are *impersonal*: rock, fortress, shield . . .

Each of these images repays unhurried meditation, and the trick is to extract from each picture, *one* key quality. God exhibits the power of a great king; the sense of justice

belonging to a just judge; and the practical care of a good shepherd. He also possesses the indestructibility of a rock; the strength of a fortress; the protective power of a shield.

So at first sight it looks as though the Bible encourages us to think of God as It, as well as He. But a closer look makes this seem less probable. For when properly used, these images do not lead us to think of God as lifeless and inert. It is the stability, strength and dependability of God to which they point, and these are *personal* attributes. Which is why Jesus called Peter 'the rock' on which he would build his Church (Matt. 16:18). He was not suggesting that Peter was a lifeless lump! Quite the reverse. He would grow into a mature person, who would be truly dependable and . . . well, rock-like![3]

Still the unease continues -- for surely God is much *more* than a person. Here I would strongly agree. We are right to be nervous of personal words if they seem to cut God down to our size. The trouble with *im*personal words is that they can reduce Him even further – to a kind of unfeeling force or power. By using personal terms, we are pointing to the

---

[3] Petros literally means 'rock' in Greek.

fact that God is more, much more, than that. God loves; He wills; He desires; He acts. And all these are *personal* attributes. True, He is described sometimes as a strong *im*personal force – for example, as 'a wind' in St John's Gospel (3:8). But unlike ordinary wind, the Spirit of God *chooses* when and where to blow.

I find it helpful to turn the problem on its head. In using personal words like Father and Shepherd, and personal pronouns like He and Him, we are not cutting God down to our size. Rather, *He alone* has these personal qualities in abundant measure. Earthly fathers and shepherds are able to reflect something of His care – because He sheds the light of His love into their hearts. God is much greater than our limited personal terms will allow – but these words do point in the right direction.

To guard against reducing God to our stature, some authors use ugly words like 'supra-personal'. In this way they acknowledge that personal terms take us down the road of understanding. At the same time they stress that such words are extremely inadequate to describe the full reality of God, who is beyond our power to describe. *No* human language can do justice to His greatness and majesty, but personal terms get a bit nearer than anything else.

4 The case for using none of these terms

Some believers, aware of the inability of language to capture the Supreme Reality, bid us to be silent. *No* words are adequate. As St Paul reminds us, 'we see through a glass darkly'. To attempt to draw word-pictures of God is as foolish as trying to paint pictures of Him on a canvas. It cannot be done; it is like trying to catch sunshine in a bottle. All we can say is that God is *not* like this, and that He is *greater* than that.

This is an important emphasis. God is greater – much greater – than our imaginations. Symbols and images are essential – but all symbols fall short of the reality, and some images can mislead. These truths are underlined in the Bible by the fact that the Israelites were forbidden to make graven images. So that nation poured its creative genius into architecture and words, rather than into pictorial art.

One important Old Testament symbol for the presence of God was the Shekinah – the cloud which mercifully shielded human eyes from the glory of God. It is significant, too, that when Roman soldiers entered the temple in Jerusalem (in AD 70), they found no representation of God in the holy of holies.

All this is an important corrective to glib statements and shallow understanding. But . . . the 'but' points to two problems. First, we cannot think about God at all without using pictures of some kind. For it is almost impossible to think without images. This applies in sophisticated physics just as it does in religion – as recently invented phrases like 'black holes in space' and 'gluons' (for subatomic particles) suggest. If we throw personal images out of the front door, other pictures will come in through the back door – inadequate pictures like 'a great force'. I read of someone who, in attempting to rid her mind of personal images in childhood, came to think of God as a vast tapioca pudding. The trouble was – she couldn't stand tapioca!

The correct way forward is not to say nothing. We shall be wiser to recognise that *all* language is inadequate, and to acknowledge that some word-pictures are better than others. In particular, we are wise to cherish those terms used by Jesus himself: words like Shepherd, King, and Father. Of course this can yield crude results. But I don't worry if people *do* think of God as an old man with a beard, provided they draw the correct conclusions. Provided 'old' suggests wisdom and eternity, rather than frailty and bewilderment.

To summarise: yes we *can* think of God as 'She' and 'It' for certain limited purposes. But we should not jettison our personal masculine pictures of God, which still carry great authority and force. I shall continue to use the pronoun 'He' when referring to God. And I shall continue to think of God as my heavenly Father. For these terms are deeply rooted in the Bible and in Christian tradition. And while it is necessary to scrutinise our tradition from time to time, we are not at liberty to abandon it – especially when it comes with the authority of Jesus himself.

POSTSCRIPT

1 *A discussion starter*. A girl volunteered to lead a discussion group which was sometimes a bit 'stodgy'. She arrived with several pieces of different coloured cloth and asked people to pick out a colour which represented the way they felt about themselves. Having done that, she asked them to select a colour which best represented the way they felt about God. The result was an open and honest discussion about faith and life. Try it!

2 *A famous vision*. 'Our Lord . . . showed me a little thing, the quantity of a hazel-nut in the palm of my hand; and it was as round as a ball. I thought thereupon with the eye of my understanding, and thought, what may this be? And it was generally answered thus: It is all that is made – I marvelled how it might last, for methought it might suddenly have fallen to nought, for littleness. And I was answered: It lasteth, and ever shall last, for God loveth it. God made it; God loveth it; God keepeth it.' *Revelations of Divine Love*; Mother Julian of Norwich (c. 1343 to 1443).

3 *Youthful wisdom*. A child drew a picture and told her teacher that it was God. The teacher said, 'But no one has ever seen God.' To this the girl replied, 'Well you have now!' Yes, we have now. For 'the Word became flesh and dwelt among us, full of grace and truth' (John 1:14 RSV).

Note to tired readers
Section 1 (page 145) of the next chapter is rather like an extended Bible study. If you are reading this at the end of a long hard day you might prefer to skip to Section 2 (page 149). Don't forget to go back to Section 1 at the weekend!

17

DO ALL RELIGIONS LEAD TO GOD?

I suspect that few authors write every chapter in the order in which they finally appear in print. Some passages flow easily from the pen or word processor and, on reflection, others are better placed in a different spot from that originally envisaged. So although we are three chapters from the end, this is the last one I wrote – mainly because I found it the hardest!

We live in a plural world where people hold a wide variety of beliefs. Agnostics and Jews rub shoulders with Christians and communists – and if we live in certain parts of Europe or America, we all rub shoulders with 'ethnic minorities'. In Britain today there are more Muslims than Methodists, and many of us pass a mosque, a synagogue or a temple every day. So the question presses hard: how do the various religions relate to one another? I am writing as a Christian about the Christian God, but I cannot duck these questions. What about other religions? Do they all ultimately lead to the same God? Is authentic experience of God to be found within them? Can we learn from members of other faiths?

The world's many religions vary considerably in their approach to one another. Some believers are convinced that theirs is the one true faith. I recall visiting a mosque and talking with a man who was quite sure that Islam is true, without remainder. As far as he was concerned, other faiths (like Christianity) have some insights, insofar as they overlap with the teaching of the Koran. Apart from that they are quite simply wrong.

So Islam is one of the great missionary religions – attempting with considerable vigour to convince non-Muslims of the truth of its doctrines. Other religions – like Hinduism and Judaism – are much less militant. They are

quietly confident of their own truths, but not particularly keen to make converts. Hindus are happy to absorb ideas from other faiths in a very tolerant manner; and to be a Jew in the full sense is a matter of birth.

Christians can be found at almost any point along that hard/soft spectrum. Some are very clear in their views. Only Christianity leads to God, to salvation, to heaven and to eternal life. All other faiths are of the devil. Even when they appear to share Christian values or concerns, other religions are deeply suspect, for the devil can masquerade as an angel of light. So Christians must evangelise vigorously, and members of other faiths must be converted or condemned to hell.

Some others take the opposite viewpoint. Live and let live. There is only one God and all religions lead to him eventually. Jesus is very significant, but God has revealed himself in different ways within different cultures. Authentic religious experiences are found equally within all the great faiths. Relax. If missionary activity continues to be valid at all, it is in helping the Jew to become a better Jew, and the Hindu to become a better Hindu.

It is because of this Babel of opinions that I am hesitant to speak. But it is impossible to write a book on the subject of

God in the modern world without addressing the problem.
So here goes . . . I am clear about two key points.

1 We must wrestle with our own faith

For Christians this means discussing, thinking and praying
within the fellowship of the Church. In particular we must
make sense of the Bible teaching on this question – and the
first part of this chapter grapples with that.

(a) *Exclusive Bible passages*. When we turn to the Bible
we find some passages which appear to be clear and exclusive. The Fourth Gospel reports the teaching of Jesus like
this: 'I am the way and the truth and the life. No-one comes
to the Father except through me' (John 14:6). In the Acts of
the Apostles Peter affirms that salvation is to be found in
Jesus and in 'no other name under heaven' (Acts 4:12).

I will make two comments on these verses. *First*, when
we examine the context of these declarations, we see that
they don't really have our question in mind. Both are firmly
set within the life of the early Church and within a Jewish
culture. The alternative on offer is not another faith –
different from the one in which the hearers have been
brought up. Their question was not: how does Christianity
relate to other religions? The burning question for them
was: will the Jews accept Jesus as the true culmination of
their own tradition?

Second, these passages do not rule out the possibility that
a person might come to the one true God through Jesus,
even though he/she does not adopt a full-blooded Christian
position. In other words, these passages insist that Jesus is
the only Saviour; they do not tell us that only Christians will
be saved. To encourage this line of thought we note that
Jesus said: '. . . whoever is not against us is for us' (Mark
9:40). To discourage it we note that he also said: 'He who is
not with me is against me' (Luke 11:23)!

Of course, some passages strongly suggest that belief in
Jesus is essential for salvation. Often (always?) these
passages have in mind those people who know who Jesus is,
and what he stands for. To know about Jesus and to remain
indifferent to him is very serious indeed – but today this is

mainly a challenge to nominal Christians, not to men and
women from non-Christian cultures. (We shall take up this
point in Chapter 19.)

(b) *Inclusive Bible passages*. Some passages in the Bible
appear to suggest that God is at work in every single human
being, regardless of background and belief. If this is true,
then all of us will be judged by the way in which we use (or
ignore) the light which we have been given.

In the prologue to the Fourth Gospel, St John says that
Jesus, the Word of God, gives light to every single person
without exception (John 1:9). St Paul expresses much the
same thought in his letter to the Romans. He speaks of
conscience, and says that those who follow its dictates find
that it accuses *or perhaps excuses (or defends) them*. Confronted with pagan worship at Lystra, Paul states that God
has provided testimony to his love for all nations – even to
those who had not heard of the prophets, nor of Jesus (Acts
14:17). At Athens he appears to go even further. Paul says
that God created the nations 'so that men would seek him
and perhaps reach out for him and find him' (Acts 17:27).

Peter lends his weight to these other apostles when
preaching in the house of Cornelius. 'I now realise how true
it is that God does not show favouritism but accepts men
from every nation who fear him and do what is right' (Acts
10:34–5). At these points the New Testament appears to
say that if we respond to the light which God gives us, then
we shall be secure even if we have never heard the name of
Jesus.

At first sight this seems very easy-going, for it sounds as
though these apostles are saying that good non-Christians
can save themselves. Probe deeper and we see that this is
not the case. For the New Testament writers are gloomy
about our willingness to respond to the 'general revelation'
of God's love and faithfulness in nature. They are even
gloomier about our ability to keep God's commandments –
whether they come in the form of written laws, or laws
written on the conscience. Indeed, we sometimes find a
very black picture. 'Once you were alienated from God and
were enemies in your minds because of your evil behaviour'
(Col. 1:21). It was *this* desperate situation which God took

by the scruff of the neck and transformed in Christ.

It is easy to be sentimental about the 'good pagan' who eagerly seeks God and truth. No doubt some do, but most non-Christians are probably like us – they find the light of God too searching for comfort and prefer an easier path.[1] The apostles make it clear that if a person who does not know the Gospel is to be saved, it can only be on the same basis as everyone else: by repenting; by accepting the grace and mercy of God; and by the saving activity of Jesus.

'. . . for all have sinned and fall short of the glory of God' (Rom. 3:23). It is only possible for *any* of us to enter heaven because God's Son has opened wide the gates of glory. The question raised by these Bible passages is not whether we can save ourselves (*no one* can), but whether God will bar the way for all except those who acknowledge Jesus as Lord in an explicit manner.

(c) *Summary and further discussion.* Some Bible passages seem hard on those who have not heard the good news of Jesus. But the really harsh sayings are reserved for those who *have* heard, but refuse to repent and obey. (If you want to follow up these ideas, I suggest Rom. 1–3; 1 Thess. 2:13–16; Heb. 2:1–4; 2 Pet. 2; 1 John 2:3–6. Also Chapter 19 of this book.) The more knowledgeable we are about the Christian way, the more will be expected of us. Conversely, Jesus was delighted when he found faith outside the Covenant-people of God (Mark 7:24–30).

God so loved *the world* that he gave his only Son, declares the most famous verse in the Bible (John 3:16). It is clear that God's purposes are for the *whole world*, not just for Christendom. Even in Old Testament times, when he was preparing his people for their worldwide mission, God used people who stood outside the community of faith: King Cyrus for example (Isa. 45). And it is surprising (but thought-provoking) to find Elisha – who could be very fierce indeed – being very gentle with Naaman, the Syrian commander. Having been healed by the living God,

---

[1] Mark Twain (?) spoke for most of us when he said: 'It is not the parts of the Scripture that I don't understand that worry me; it is the parts that I do understand.' As H. G. Wells put it: 'To this day this Galilean is too much for our small hearts.'

Naaman asked permission to continue with one of his pagan practices, and Elisha told him to 'Go in peace' (2 Kgs. 5:18–19).

In his approach to pagan audiences, St Paul declares that God has overlooked earlier sins, now that the new age has dawned (Acts 17:30). True, he makes it clear that the time for such 'laxity' has passed for his hearers, and that God wants all people, everywhere, to repent. But if God judged earlier generations according to the limited light which they possessed, we can ask a question. Might not God continue to make every allowance in those parts of the world where the Gospel is not yet preached – or where the cultural background makes it very difficult to hear the good news for what it is (partly as a result of unChristian behaviour by Christians)? Perhaps this was implied by Peter and Paul in the verses quoted earlier (Acts 10:34, 35 and 17:27).

I could produce further passages from the Bible and raise more questions, but I won't – for I readily concede that it is very hard to prove conclusively any one viewpoint in this area. This is a subject where Christians sometimes disagree. For the teaching of the Bible contains various strands which are relevant to the important question: Do all religions lead to God? It is tempting to pick and choose those verses which we find most congenial, or most supportive of our particular viewpoint.

But I am clear about three points. First, we *all* need to be rescued or saved by the initiative and grace of God. There is no such thing as a do-it-yourself salvation kit. Second, God 'wants *all men* [my italics] to be saved and to come to a knowledge of the truth' (1 Tim. 2:4; see also 2 Pet. 3:9). Third, some Bible teaching presents us with a more gentle picture of God in relation to those of other faiths, than could be guessed at when we listen to some Christians. We worship the God who is love (1 John 4:16). I for one am content to accept the Psalmist's assurance that God will judge 'uprightly' (Ps. 75:2). We shall be wise to hold Abraham's question in mind: 'Will not the Judge of all the earth do right?' (Gen. 18:25).

A Christless Eternity? Recently I received literature from a missionary society, which spoke of those who have not heard of Jesus going to 'a Christless eternity'. I am not so sure. What *is* clear is that we must take the judgment of God very seriously. This applies particularly to those of us who *do* know the Christian message, for those who choose to ignore Jesus are in great spiritual danger. Those who appear to follow him, but who are in fact doing no such thing, are in greater danger still (Matt. 25:31–46). Perhaps it is these who will go to 'a Christless eternity'.

The position of those who have not heard the good news of Jesus is not directly tackled in any depth in the New Testament. What is made clear is that every single human being will be judged by a holy, merciful and all-knowing God. The warning bells do not announce that those who have not heard the good news of Jesus will perish. Rather, they declare that it is those who *have* heard (you and me) who are in the greatest peril. An urgent response is required: repent and believe the Gospel. For 'how shall we escape if we ignore such a great salvation?' (Heb. 2:3).

2   We must relate our faith to other faiths

We can avoid the need for this by sealing ourselves off from contact with people who hold other beliefs, but this is increasingly difficult in the modern world. I suggest that three qualities should mark any approach by Christians to those who differ from them.

(a) *Courtesy and humility*. Christianity has a pretty poor record in relation to people of other faiths. Some of our forefathers were models of Christian courtesy and love – but many baptised by force and persecuted those who refused to submit. We have a lot to live down, for memories are long. For example, in the ancient city of York there is no synagogue, possibly because Jews will not settle in large numbers in a city which persecuted them 800 years ago. I believe that we must work hard to heal these wounds, by openly admitting our offences and by listening carefully to what others have to say to us. Such honesty will be painful, but it is necessary and right.

In particular, we need to judge other faiths by their best practices and practitioners. It is all too easy to highlight unpleasant and superstitious aspects of other religions, while hoping that they will judge us according to our best examples. If people judge Christianity by speaking of the violence of the IRA, or of their Protestant counterparts in Northern Ireland, we get hot under the collar. We protest that this is not what Christianity is about. We ask for accurate assessment. In the same way we must be generous when we assess the beliefs, practices and religious experiences of other faiths.

It is important for us to seek common ground. When St Paul visited Athens (Acts 17) he was disturbed at the pagan religion which he observed. He desperately wanted to tell those Gentiles about the risen Lord. But when he spoke, he did his utmost to build bridges. He highlighted differences, but he also spoke as positively as possible about the religious viewpoints and practices of his hearers, and quoted (with approval) their own religious poetry. He then went on to share his own faith with them.

(b) *Honesty*. As we talk and listen with those of other faiths we shall realise that we have a fair amount in common. Obvious examples are the stress upon prayer and alms-giving. Other examples are mystical experiences and speaking in tongues (which are by no means confined to Christianity), and some shared emphases. The following extracts would sit comfortably within the Christian tradition.

> Never in this world is hate
> Appeased by hatred;
> It is only appeased by love –
> This is the eternal law
>   (Gautama, the Buddha).

By the light of day, and by the fall of night, your Lord
    has not forsaken you, nor does He abhor you.
The life to come holds a richer prize for you than this
    present life.
You shall be gratified with what your Lord will.
    Did He not find you an orphan and give you shelter?
    Did He not find you in error and guide you?

Did He not find you poor and enrich you?
Therefore do not wrong the orphan, nor chide away the
beggar. But proclaim the goodness of your Lord.
The Koran (sometimes written as Qür'an).

If men thought of God as much as they think of the
world, who would not attain liberation?
From *The Maitri Upanishad.*

Honesty compels us to notice the *differences* between the
various world religions too. Some people are sentimental
and blinkered, and pretend that they all appear to be saying
the same thing. This is far from true – a point which John
Polkinghorne makes with considerable clarity:

Having gladly paid tribute to the authenticity of religious
experience outside the acknowledged confines of Christianity, I want to go on to say as my second point that it
would be a grave mistake to suppose that there are no
significant differences between the world religions. Their
views of the world certainly differ. For example, it seems
to me that the religions originating in the Near East
(Judaism, Christianity, Islam) have a more realistic view
of the world and the evil in it than do the religions of the
Far East. I cannot accept that the suffering of the world
is an illusion from which release is to be sought by
enlightenment. Rather, the cross of Christ demonstrates
the objective and inescapable character of that suffering.
A Buddhist might find a crucifix an ugly and degrading
symbol of suffering. I believe that on the cross Jesus
opened his arms to embrace the bitterness of the world.
   Above all there is the fundamental difference between
Christianity and other religions about the significance of
Jesus. (From *The Way the World Is*: SPCK, 1983).

It is for this reason that I have strong reservations about
multifaith services. I am delighted to talk with, and listen'
to, non-Christian friends. I am eager to work with them on
social issues for which we have a common concern. And I
am keen to pray alongside them in certain circumstances.
For example, in northern England on May 11th, 1985, a

terrible fire engulfed Bradford's football ground. Many people were killed or injured. On such an occasion, men and women of all faiths and none must draw together – to express grief and mutual support, and to provide opportunity for prayers to be offered by those who believe in prayer.

This is quite different from arranging multifaith services without such a springboard. Such services can blur important distinctions and give false impressions. Usually, the blandest of Scriptures are chosen, the most general prayers are offered, and the notion of Jesus as *the* mediator between us and God is soft-pedalled. If we do meet in this way, I suggest that we might keep silence together, rather than compromise our distinctiveness.

(c) *Boldness*. When we have done all the courteous listening that we can, we shall want to do some speaking as well. And many adherents of other faiths will want us to do so. For they will not have much respect for us, unless the light of our own faith burns strongly within us, as theirs does within them. True faith must lead to action – and to speech. Christianity is one of the world's great missionary religions. We are called to preach the Gospel and to share our faith.

This does not overrule the previous few paragraphs, for evangelism does not mean forcing our views on other people. As D. T. Niles, a great Asian Christian, put it – evangelism is a question of one beggar showing another beggar where he found bread. We have *good news*. Let us share it!

Our witness will focus upon the person of Jesus. We shall want to point our non-Christian friends to him, for he alone rose from the dead. He alone is King of Kings. He alone is Lord and Saviour as well as teacher and prophet. This is the Christian conviction, which can more readily find a place within dialogue, discussion and proclamation than in multifaith worship.

This stress on Jesus has been called 'the scandal of particularity'. We insist that if Muslims or Buddhists are to experience God, and to be saved, it is not through any mediator but Jesus (whether they recognise him or not).

For he alone is the Saviour *of the world*. '. . . there is no other name under heaven given to men by which we must be saved' (Acts 4:12). This is a hard saying. But it is not negotiable.

Conclusion. No doubt some readers will strongly disagree with the contents of this chapter. To some I shall seem far too easy-going – appearing to compromise the need to preach the Gospel with urgency and conviction. To others I shall seem very harsh: an arrogant Christian who claims that only his faith is ultimately true and satisfying.

So be it. I do not claim to have all the answers, by any means. If others can persuade me that my approach is flawed, I will gladly listen. But I hope that this chapter will lead some readers back to the Bible to do some hard studying, and on to bookshops and libraries to read better books on the subject. To this end I list some suggestions below.[2]

We cannot simply read off easy answers in the Bible, for the answers are not easy. But we can study, pray, and think hard – and we can attempt to make sure that our studies spill over into friendship with those of other faiths. For there is nothing so challenging and broadening as actually *meeting* people who hold other viewpoints and beliefs, with conviction and clarity. It is by this means that caricatures disappear, and preconceived ideas evaporate.

And so we return to our original question. Do all religions lead to God? No. Not even Christianity. Only Jesus Christ does that. Jesus who promised, 'seek and you will find', and who prayed for his pagan tormentors, 'Father, forgive them, for they do not know what they are doing' (Luke 23:34). I for one do not doubt that his prayer was answered with a resounding 'Yes'. In closing – a simple but profound illustration. I asked the Lord, 'How much do you love us?' To answer, he stretched out his arms on the cross, to embrace the whole world.

---

[2] On the subject of the Christian faith in relation to other faiths, I find books by Norman Anderson, Kenneth Cragg, Stephen Neill and Lesslie Newbigin very helpful. John Polkinghorne's book *The Way The World Is* (SPCK, 1983) is also well worth reading. Chapter 10 (quoted above) looks at this subject. Also useful is Keith Ward's *The Turn of the Tide* (BBC, 1986): see *Postscript*.

POSTSCRIPT

1   *Who needs a missionary?* I recall a lecture by Bishop Lesslie Newbigin, in which he referred to his experience of settling into Britain again, following missionary work in South India. He said that he found Britain a much tougher mission field than India, where people are more open to God, and where religious questions are taken seriously.

2   *An important distinction.* 'It seems to me what we have to do is distinguish two things quite clearly. We must separate the question of what is true or false from the question of how a person can be saved . . . This does not at all mean that it does not matter what you believe; as if, since you will be saved anyway, you can believe anything you like. The doctrine is that you can be saved only if you respond fully and openly to the truth as you perceive it. It does matter that you seek the truth. We might say: you will be judged by how seriously you have sought the truth; but you will not be judged on whether you have actually found it or not'. Keith Ward in *Turn of the Tide*.

3   *An endorsement.* A somewhat similar approach can be found in *The Last Battle*, by C. S. Lewis (the seventh and last of his Narnia stories for children). Also in *Christianity and Comparative Religion* (IVP, 1970)[3] by Professor Sir Norman Anderson. He insists that no one can 'earn salvation'. But he points to verses like Matthew 7:7 ('seek and you will find') and Proverbs 8:17, which assures us that 'those who seek me find me.' He argues that other faiths contain genuine insights. ('I have never met a Muslim convert who regards the God he previously sought to worship as a totally false God.') And he asserts his belief that a non-Christian who throws himself on the mercy of God 'would find that mercy – although without understanding it – at the cross on which "Christ died for all"'. But Norman Anderson does not undervalue the great commis-

---

[3] Revised and reissued in 1984 as *Christianity and World Religions* (IVP). This is an excellent starting-point for further reading – and gives an extensive list of other books on this subject.

sion given by Jesus, for we are under orders (Matt. 28:20).
He quotes Bishop Lesslie Newbigin as follows.

4 *A challenge*. 'The Church does not apologise for the fact
that it wants all men to know Jesus Christ and to follow him.
Its very calling is to proclaim the Gospel to the ends of the
earth. It cannot make any restrictions in this respect'
Lesslie Newbigin, *The Finality of Christ* (SCM, 1969).

5 *A hope*. 'But what will be the fate of those who have
never heard? If we grant that human beings left to themselves are perishing, and that they cannot save themselves,
and that Jesus is the only qualified saviour . . . what
condition has to be fulfilled in order that they may be
saved? Is there any way in which God will have mercy on
them?

'Speaking for myself, I believe the most Christian stance
is to remain agnostic on this question. But I am imbued with
hope. I hope that the majority of the human race will be
saved. And I have a solid biblical basis for this belief.' John
Stott, Rector Emeritus: All Souls' Church, Langham
Place, London, in *Essentials* (Hodder, 1988).

6 *A summary*. 'For the human sickness there is one
specific remedy, and this is it. There is no other.' Bishop
Stephen Neill, writing about the life, death and resurrection of Jesus.

The Collect for the ninth Sunday before Easter
Eternal God, whose son Jesus Christ is for all mankind the
way, the truth, and the life: grant us to walk in his way, to
rejoice in his truth, and to share his risen life; who is alive
and reigns with you and the Holy Spirit, one God, now and
for ever.

Part 4

THE WRATH OF GOD

Hell is other people
Jean-Paul Sartre

Hell is oneself
T. S. Eliot

For although they knew God, they neither glorified him as
God nor gave thanks to him, but their thinking became
futile and their foolish hearts were darkened.
St Paul (Rom. 1:21)

18

ANGRY JUDGE

During the past few years certain events have caused some people to ask whether God has intervened in judgment in human affairs. I shall select two examples. One of these was a fire; the other is a plague. The former was a relatively local event – though distressing to many people around the world. The latter is the most serious health problem to appear on the world stage in modern times. I am referring to the fire which damaged York Minster, and to the scourge of AIDS (Acquired Immune Deficiency Syndrome). Two very different events, with one thing in common: both have been used as evidence for the judgment of God on human wickedness. Let's look at them a little more closely.

In the early morning of July 9th, 1984, a fire did great damage to the south transept of York Minster. Some people saw the fire as an act of God – not in the sense in which that phrase is used in insurance contracts, but, quite literally, as an act of divine judgment. Indeed, during a church service broadcast on BBC radio a few weeks later, one man said that the event had been decisive in bringing him to faith in God!

Such views were strongly condemned by others, including some church leaders. Vigorous debate ensued. We live in York so I followed the argument with great interest. It ran like this . . . A few weeks before the fire, it was announced that the next bishop of Durham would be a professor of theology from Leeds University. The announcement caused no ripples, for few people outside academic or church circles had heard of David Jenkins.

That soon changed! The bishop-to-be appeared on television and made the kind of pronouncements which

journalists love. In particular, he appeared to cast doubt on
the virgin birth and the resurrection of Jesus. Although he
often reaffirmed his belief in the resurrection, there was an
outcry. For bishops are required to defend the faith, not
to attack it. So the Archbishop of York was lobbied with
requests that the professor should not be consecrated
as bishop, unless he first made a full public declaration
of his Christian faith. The Archbishop refused this
demand, and the consecration went ahead in York
Minster.

The new bishop seemed to enjoy himself. He appeared
frequently on radio and television. Christianity was on
the agenda in many a pub, and David Jenkins claimed
this as a success, for he wanted people to think for
themselves. Six days after his consecration, the Minster
fire broke out and the debate took a new turn. Was it,
or was it not, the judgment of God on the Church of
England?

Compared with the next problem we shall consider, the
fuss over the Bishop of Durham seems like a merry romp
through *Barchester Towers*. When the York fire occurred in
the summer of 1984, few people had heard of AIDS. Now it
is a household word. The disease spread rapidly through
homosexual communities in America and Britain (hence it

was offensively described by some as 'the gay plague'). In Africa it has killed thousands of heterosexual men and women, and it continues to spread at a terrifying rate. In January 1988 an international conference on AIDS was organised by the World Health Organisation. One expert predicted that one million people will have the disease by 1991. It was described as 'a threat to humanity'.

As with the fire, so with the disease: some Christians were not slow to see this as the judgment of God upon a sinful world. In the face of that interpretation of events, what are we to say? I shall make four points.

1 *The living God*. Christians are committed to the belief that God is living and active. In particular, Christmas, Easter and Pentecost are powerful reminders of the fact that God has intervened decisively in human affairs. But it would be quite wrong to suppose that God's involvement in his world is past and over. For Jesus promised that he would be with his disciples until the end of time. We ask for God's intervention and involvement every time we pray for the sick, the dying and the lonely. We worship the *living God*.

He is also the sovereign Lord. We know from his many glorious promises, that his purposes for us are good. But his ways with us are often mysterious and hard to understand.

2 *A consuming fire*. We are taught in the New Testament that 'God is love' (1 John 4:8). But this does not rule out judgment. In his first letter to the Corinthians – only two chapters before the famous passage on love (13) – Paul refers to this other side of the coin. He reminds the Christians at Corinth of the need to receive Holy Communion only after thorough and careful preparation. Because they failed to do this, some members of the early Church had fallen ill; indeed some of them had died (1 Cor. 11:30). We can, if we choose, dismiss this as outdated superstition. Personally, I should prefer to learn the solemn lessons which that passage conveys. God can, and sometimes does, act in judgment – and he starts with the Church.

The same truth is illustrated even more startlingly in the

Acts of the Apostles. Throughout Luke's account of the early days of the Church, we see the dynamic action of God's Spirit bringing faith, courage and love to many lives. But God was active in judgment too. The Church was tiny and vulnerable. The early Christians had no weapons but their conviction that God had raised Jesus from the dead, and the quality of their lives. It was vital that they should be open and honest with one another. Otherwise, what persecution could not achieve, inner corruption might. So when a married couple lied to their fellow-believers, they were struck dead (Acts 5:1–11).

To many modern Christians that passage is extremely difficult and embarrassing. But it stands to this day as a warning. As the writer of the letter to the Hebrews put it, 'our God is a consuming fire' (12:29). The early believers came to see from the teaching of Jesus that three attitudes to God were required of them. They were to *trust* God. In this regard they were to think of God as Father – or even as friend. They were to *love* God. And they were to *fear* God: not with a cringing fear, but with the deep reverence, awe and respect which is due to the Holy One who is our Creator and Saviour.

There is a lovely illustration of this in the Narnia stories of C. S. Lewis. Aslan the lion (who is the Christ-figure in the stories) romps and plays with the children – but always present is an unpredictable edge of greatness and mystery. They may play with him at his invitation; they must not get *too* familiar.

So we must beware of assuming too readily that we modern Christians can predict the ways of God with humankind. He acted in judgment in the past; he can do so again. Some church leaders appeared unwilling to entertain the faintest possibility that God might be responsible for the fire at York Minster. Some of them seemed to be sure about this, because in their view God is not like that, and would not behave in that way. But this comes close to denying the strand of judgment which runs not only through the Old Testament, but through the New as well. Besides, even if God did not cause the fire, he could (and did, I believe) speak through it. The debate which followed David Jenkins' consecration was undoubtedly 'fuelled' (literally: forgive the pun) by the fire. And one result of that debate was that many bishops re-examined their role as teachers of the faith, and pastors and encouragers of the faithful.

Mind you, I don't believe that God *did* cause the York fire. If he did, then his timing isn't very good! For the fire happened several days after the service of consecration. No: if God wanted to make a point, I suspect that he would have timed it more accurately! In any case, I do not think that David Jenkins is a terrible sinner, deserving of such special treatment. True, he can be harsh and uncharitable towards orthodox Christians with whom he disagrees (people like me!). He accuses us of worshipping 'a cultic idol' or 'the very devil' – very serious and hurtful accusations. And he is sometimes muddled in his thinking. Richard Harries (Bishop of Oxford) shows this with his convincing arguments against David Jenkins' position in *Christ is Risen* (Mowbray 1987). Despite this, the Bishop of Durham can inspire deep trust in the living God. Consider this extract from his recent book:

For my part, I am quite clear that miracles occur. I am clear about this because I am part of the community who believes in God through Jesus Christ and because of my personal experience, conviction and commitment. But I am equally clear that I do not believe in God nor in his Son Jesus Christ our Lord because of miracles. Because God is there and because God is active and God is loving, and because I and all my fellow human beings are potentially open and free beings in the image of God, there is no telling what wonderful signs, intimations and gifts are to be received in the gracious and mysterious dealings between God and men and women in this world. But one thing is clear. God will not deny himself as he has shown himself to be in Jesus Christ. We may be sure therefore that miracles are not proofs of power but gifts of love to be received by faith. Further, they are to be responded to in life and by praising and by trusting God, whether he gives us more miracles or whether he does not (*God, Miracle and the Church of England*, SCM, 1987).

3 *Two kinds of judgment.* If David Jenkins needs to learn humility, then some of his critics need to learn a similar lesson. For it is a serious thing to claim that God is acting in judgment on someone else. This is particularly true of some statements about the spread of AIDS.

Many Christians have stressed the need for compassion and practical help for the victims. Others, like Hugh Montefiore (the recently retired Bishop of Birmingham) have gone on to point out that there is only one way to stop the spread of AIDS in its tracks. To do this we must press for a return to traditional Christian morality: faithfulness within marriage and chastity outside marriage. But, in addition to these responses, some have spoken with considerable confidence and vehemence of the disease of AIDS as the judgment of God – especially upon the homosexual community.

We need to use such language with great caution. I do not believe that God has picked out certain individuals to afflict with the AIDS virus, as a punishment for their sins (see Postscript: page 167). And it is clear that one of the great tragedies of the scourge has been the infection of innocent people through blood transfusions. Mercifully, that particular source of infection was quickly detected and stemmed in most countries.

But perhaps we can and should speak of God's judgment upon the human race through AIDS in a *general* sense. The Bible is clear: sexual exploitation and promiscuity are wrong (homosexual *and* heterosexual), and to ignore this teaching brings its own judgment. This is not to say, of course, that all who suffer from AIDS have been sexually promiscuous. Tragically, a single act of sexual intercourse can be 'enough'. But any such victim is likely to be at the end of a long chain of tangled sexual encounters.

In the Bible, God's judgment on sin is seen in two ways. First, as direct intervention in punishment – as in the case of Ananias and Sapphira mentioned above (Acts 5:1–11). But there is a more subtle means of judgment, too. In the early chapters of his letter to the Romans, St Paul catalogues many of the sins which were common in the Roman Empire, and which continue to be widespread today.

He goes on to speak about God's judgment in a rather surprising way.

God's response to all this was not a thunderbolt from heaven. Instead, we read that 'he gave them up' to the consequences of their chosen way of life. We are to understand from this that if we continue to ignore God's laws and guidelines, then certain consequences will inevitably follow – for that is the way the world is. These truths about judgment were put powerfully by Archbishop Michael Ramsey in a famous book written well before the onset of AIDS:

> Here I would suggest the beginning of our answer. Recall a biblical doctrine too often forgotten, the doctrine of divine judgement. When men and nations turn away from God's laws and prefer the courses dictated by pride and selfishness to the courses dictated by conscience, calamitous results follow. God is not absent from the contemporary scene; he is present, present in judgement through the catastrophes which follow human wilfulness . . . And as the judgement of God is accepted and felt, so in the same moment may his loving kindness and mercy be found . . . Let it however be remembered that divine judgement falls first upon God's people the Church . . . The Church shows the message of divine judgement to the world as she sees the judgement upon herself and begins to mend her ways (*The Christian Priest Today*: SPCK, revised 1985).

4 *Love is supreme*. Michael Ramsey's reminder about loving kindness is an important note on which to end this chapter. Christians are called to love the sinner while hating his or her sin. This can be a cliché and it is certainly difficult to achieve. But it is an attitude which is found consistently in the ministry and teaching of Jesus himself. Indeed, it was *because* he loved people that he hated their sins. For he realised that sin is like a poison in the body, and he longed that men and women should be set free to experience wholeness, fulfilment, self-control and – in the long run – happiness.

So Jesus did not condemn the woman caught in adultery, but he did instruct her to 'go and sin no more'. Instead of condemnation – a challenge to purity of life. For that way, and that way alone, would lead to her fulfilment as a person, rather than her non-fulfilment as an exploited sexual object.

In the light of AIDS, the Church is called to face a twofold challenge. We must show a deep and costly love for the victims of that terrible disease. My prayer is that many Christians will befriend, hug, and welcome AIDS sufferers into their homes. But we face a tougher challenge, too. I have spent much of my life working among young people. For most of them the true alternative to Christian faith is not Buddhism or agnosticism or Marxism. For many young people the true alternative to Christian faith is hedonism – the love of pleasure (mixed, I joyfully concede, with various measures of idealism and political action).

The choice is between short-term pleasure which comes from sexual licence and the bottle; and long-term happiness which comes from Christ and the Church. But for many this does not seem to be a real choice. For Christianity does not appear to be an attractive alternative. So there seems to be only one way – the way of pleasure.

It is the same situation in a different guise with the older generation, too. The aim of many people in middle or old age is simply to make this year a little more comfortable than last, and next year a little more comfortable than this. So their vision of life is focused almost entirely upon their home, their neighbourhood and their holiday. It satisfies . . . after a fashion. Just occasionally, disturbing thoughts like 'I am getting old' or 'there must be more to life than this' break in.

It is not until they meet people who really *do* appear to be living joyfully – by other standards and with other aims – that they realise that there really *is* a choice on offer. It has been my privilege to see people of all ages discover and make that choice, as a result of meeting followers of Jesus. Not enough people by any means – and that is largely due to the spiritual poverty of the Church at large, and of my own individual life in particular.

Perhaps that is what St Peter means, in part at least,

when he asserts that judgment will begin with the 'household of God'. Part of the significance of that frightening statement must mean that we are not living as salt and light (the terms which Jesus used for his disciples) in that corner of the world in which God has called us to live.

No, I am not asking for 'super-saints' – simply for churches which take Jesus seriously. And for Christians who joyfully accept his release from materialism and hedonism, and whose lives present an attractive alternative to the television adverts. This is challenging, but it is not asking too much. For we have the living Christ to help us.

POSTSCRIPT ON DISASTER AND JUDGMENT

People sometimes assume that disaster is a judgment from God, and they ask, 'What have I – or what has he or she – done to deserve this?' Sometimes the answer is clear (see page 161). But usually the answer is – nothing. We are driven to this conclusion from two directions. First, we observe that fine people sometimes suffer terrible calamities. Second, we read the words of Jesus.

Nowhere does he attempt to give a 'defence' of God in the face of unjust suffering. Instead, he teaches that God's care for us is very detailed – even the hairs on our head are numbered. But he acknowledges that the natural world has a life of its own. Rain and sunshine fall on good and bad alike. And disasters befall innocent people. When a tower collapsed and killed eighteen people, he taught his hearers not to point a finger of judgment at those caught up in the tragedy. Rather, they should ponder the unpredictability of life – and repent (Luke 13:1–5).

Jesus also insists that we take an eternal perspective. Death is not the ultimate tragedy, for death is not the end of us. This is unpopular today for it sounds dangerously like 'pie in the sky when you die'. But if the sky is real, and the pie is real . . . God's way is not simple *reversal* of the bad things – but *redemption* and *resurrection*. Good Friday and Easter Sunday set the pattern. He can bring life out of death and joy out of sadness – not only in the next world, but in this world, too.

2   *Inspiring examples*. The experience of many sufferers is that God brings strength out of weakness. This is not universal and I do not pretend to understand the apparent inconsistency of God. Instead I will use the words of those who have suffered great pain, to bring this postscript to an end.

Following the death from cancer of his 21-year-old son, Professor Sir Norman Anderson wrote:

> People used continually to ask us why a young man of such promise, and with such a zest for life, should be allowed to die so young. To this the only reply, we both feel, is that we do not, and cannot, know. The vital question to ask God in such cases is not, 'Why did you allow this?' (to which he seldom, I think, vouchsafes an answer), but, 'What do you want to teach me through this?'

In *Matthew* (Highland, 1987) Bob Jackson struggles with the death of his 10-year-old son in an accident on a family holiday in Austria. He movingly and honestly charts the violent mood-swings of his family. At one point he quotes Martin Luther King: 'It's not how *long* you live, it's how *well* you live.' In conversation with his wife, he expressed his view that this is God's perspective on life, and should be ours as well. She responded, 'In my better moments that's how I see it.' (*Matthew* is well worth reading).

3   *On living joyfully*. Towards the end of this chapter I talked about people who are 'living joyfully'. I thought very hard about that little phrase. Is it honest? Does it give a true impression of my life – and of the church to which I belong?

At St Paul's we are a very mixed bunch. Ordinary people, yes – but with some remarkable stories, too. We live in the real world. Only today I have spoken to people with deep problems at home and at work. So between us we do our fair share of worrying and of difficult decision-making. We know what it is to fail, to cry, to be dejected.

But faith in God is strong – and it 'connects' with real life. And there is a great deal of mutual support and encouragement. Mixed in with the tears there is a lot of laughter. Some of us do 'live joyfully', some of the time at least. And in the bad times, we believe (with Dame Julian) that 'all shall be well' in the long run. For Jesus is Lord of life and death – and of laughter and tears, as well.

I suspect that this description fits most churches in most countries in most ages.

19

GOD WHO CASTS INTO HELL

The Bible raises another, even deeper, question concerning the judgment of God. For it sets out a glorious vision of a perfected future, when God will re-create a new heaven and a new earth. In picture, parable, and poetry we read promise after promise which amounts to this: God will perform one final great act of creation. At that moment everything will be under his direct control. There will be a new heaven and a new earth, and 'at the name of Jesus, every knee shall bow'.

The picture which is painted is glorious. The lion and the lamb will lie down together; a little child will play safely over the hole of a deadly snake. The creation which now 'groans in travail' and is marked by suffering, will be redeemed. Pain will be banished, and God will wipe every tear from every eye.

The picture is also alarming – which is why Jesus instructs us to watch and to pray. It is alarming because it contains a strong element of judgment. For an inescapable feature of the End Time will be the final separation of the sheep from the goats, as spelt out in the famous parable which Jesus told (Matt. 25:31–46). In other words, there will be a new heaven and a new earth – *and an old hell too*.

This aspect of the Christian faith is not often preached about today. This is partly for practical reasons – for preaching on this theme appears to have lost its power to influence. People continue to be very superstitious, but they only want to believe in *good* luck! So Christians are embarrassed at being thought old-fashioned and melancholy. For if heaven is not old-fashioned, hell certainly is.

But there are other reasons, too. Theological reasons. God is love: this is the clear teaching of the Bible, and that is the message which the Church rightly wishes to proclaim.

So the argument runs on . . . Surely a God who casts into hell is not a loving God? Indeed he is more like a monster. Besides, it would be a denial of his ultimate power, if he were to leave even one small corner of the universe which does not bow the knee to Jesus, for he is King of Kings and Lord of Lords. The existence of hell would thwart God's clearly stated purpose of salvation for all.

Now I have deep sympathy with all of that, and would greatly prefer to close this chapter at this point. But I can't, for (and here I want to use very, very small letters) I do believe in hell. To some readers this might suggest that I am medieval in my thinking. But to those who are prepared to read on, I shall attempt to give an explanation.

1   *Picture-language.* I readily agree that the teaching of the New Testament concerning heaven and hell is drawn in picture-language. Gehenna – the Greek word for hell in the New Testament – refers to an actual rubbish dump outside Jerusalem. The fires at Gehenna did quite literally burn by day and by night, and the worms were alive and active in that rich compost.

Gehenna was a convenient, well-known and vivid illustration. So we should not take the images literally. But neither can we remove them altogether. Clearly, they are intended to represent an undesirable and dismal state of affairs, which we should be wise to escape if we possibly can. In addition to this vivid picture of fire, rubbish dump and worms, the New Testament speaks about hell in other terms, too – as darkness, and as spiritual death and separation from God (2 Thess. 1:9). And sometimes it speaks as though we judge ourselves, by the way we respond to, or ignore, God's light and love.

2   *The teaching of Jesus.* The person in the New Testament who speaks most strongly and persistently about hell, is Jesus himself. People sometimes assume that his teaching was all sweetness and light. Then they accuse St Paul of complicating Jesus' simple message, and making it severe and unpalatable.

This is quite untrue. Jesus gave some wonderful promises, and often spoke in gentle terms – especially to those who were emotionally or physically bruised. But he was relentless in his opposition to hypocrisy, and indifference to the plight of the poor. Indeed, if there are parts of the New Testament which give any substance to the argument for universalism (the belief that everyone will ultimately be saved) they come from the pen of St Paul, not from the lips of Jesus. For example: 'For as in Adam all die, so in Christ all will be made alive' (1 Cor. 15:22).

3 *Real choices*. God is not an ogre who enjoys punishing human beings. Quite the reverse. He loves the world which he made. Indeed he loves the world so much that 'he gave his one and only Son, that whoever believes in him shall not perish but have eternal life' (John 3:16). The New Testament makes it clear that God's strong desire is that every single person should escape hell and go to heaven. For example: 'This is good, and pleases God our Saviour, who wants all men to be saved and to come to a knowledge of the truth' (1 Tim. 2:3–4). 'He is patient with you, not wanting anyone to perish, but everyone to come to repentance' (2 Pet. 3:9).

But love requires a willing response. In creating us with a real measure of freedom, God took the risk that some would spurn his love. In many ways hell is a very modern doctrine. For we hear a lot these days (from psychologists and counsellors, for example) about 'taking responsibility for ourselves'. This is precisely the position which God takes up in relation to us. He does not coerce us; he will not force us. If we prefer to refuse the light which he gives; if we continue to insist on doing our own thing in our own way; then . . . so be it.

This was clearly and grimly put by the preacher who suggested that on Judgment Day only four words will be spoken. Those who respond to God will say to him: 'Your will be done.' To those who refuse to accept his way of love, God will say the same words: 'Your will be done.' Spoken by him, they assume an awful finality.

An old Korean tale spells this out. The story concerns a man who was given a conducted tour of heaven and hell. To his surprise they were identical: huge tables covered with delicious food, and long chop-sticks. He was puzzled until he returned at dinner-time. In hell, people were trying to feed themselves, but the chop-sticks were far too long. In heaven, people were using the chop-sticks to feed one another.

We can have no very clear idea of who will be in heaven, and no doubt there will be surprises. Perhaps Hitler will be there, for no one knows whether he repented before taking poison in his bunker. But assuming for the moment that he died with the same attitudes that marked his life, then he would dislike heaven intensely. For heaven means focusing our thoughts on God, and forgetting ourselves. In heaven, love will reign supreme, and hatred will be banished. Unless he were drastically changed, Hitler would not wish to inhabit such a place, for he would be required to bow the knee to Jesus the Jew.

Such a deep change would need to take place that it would not be Hitler as we know him. It would involve a whole personality transplant. That could only take place in one of two ways – either with his willing co-operation, or by force. It seems that God refuses to take the latter path. If while we live on earth we oppose and reject all that Jesus taught and stood for, it is unlikely that we shall like his agenda in heaven any better.

Of course, each of us will find the adjustment difficult. To make it possible we shall need to be changed, and that will happen 'in a flash, in the twinkling of an eye' (1 Cor 15:52). But that change must be voluntary. God will do the transforming – but only with our permission. It is rather like signing a hospital consent form for an operation. To do so involves surgery – and life. If we withhold consent, we avoid the surgery, but we get steadily worse.

4 *Personal experience*. I believe in hell, mainly because Jesus taught about its reality. But I have another reason, too – I have personal experience of hell. Lest this sounds melodramatic I will spell out my meaning. When I look deeply into my own life and examine my own motives and responses, I am alarmed at what I find. Some generosity of spirit and concern for others, yes. I thank God for these, for I sense that they come from him. But I find other, ugly things lurking there, too: jealousy, greed, self-centredness, lust, deviousness, lack of self-control . . .

You might be inclined to reject this point, on the supposition that I am a very gloomy person, much given to unhealthy introspection. My friends assure me that I am in fact a fairly merry soul, and often outward-looking. But I have moments of severe realism, as you can discern. If you refer to pages 16/17 you will see the same self-estimate made by two other men.

This theme has been taken up in our century in two famous plays. The French atheist, Jean-Paul Sartre, set his play *In Camera* in hell. There are no instruments of torture; simply three people living together for all eternity. They irritate and agitate one another in a thousand ways. One terse sentence sums up the thrust of Sartre's play: 'Hell is other people.'

T. S. Eliot took a different line. E. Martin Browne was sitting next to Eliot at the dress-rehearsal of the latter's play, *The Cocktail Party*. When an actor spoke his equally famous line: 'Hell is oneself', T. S. Eliot turned to his friend and said, 'against Sartre'.

Perhaps these positions aren't as polarised as they appear. For without the self-centredness to which Eliot refers, the characters in Sartre's play would relate warmly and well, and they would not be in hell. But if I had to choose between them. I should be for Eliot and against Sartre in this particular debate. For I am aware that if I were to live on into eternity, and if the negative qualities which mark my inner life were left unchecked, then I should become a nightmare. If they were fed and developed, then they would consume and take me over completely. Which is another way of talking about hell.

5 *Faith and Love*. 'The path to hell is paved with good intentions.' So runs the old English proverb. But this is not quite the teaching of the Bible. According to the Christian Scriptures, the way to hell is paved with: (a) lack of faith, and (b) lack of love.

The first point is illustrated very plainly in the Fourth Gospel. In debate with the religious teachers of his day, Jesus declared: 'if you do not believe that I am the one I claim to be, you will indeed die in your sins' (John 8:24). This assertion tells us little about the eternal destiny of those millions of people around the world who have never heard of Jesus (see Chapter 17). It has everything to do with *our* situation. For Jesus was talking to people who – like us – knew very clearly what he taught, claimed and did.

To be confronted by Jesus and *still* to say that we prefer to go our own way – this is the ultimate disaster. For it means that we shall 'die in our sins'. The only proper response – and like it or not, the only *safe* response – is to accept and follow him. Which is what 'belief' means in St John's writings. For faith is an active and dynamic concept. It involves entrusting our lives to God, and basing our behaviour on the teaching and example of Jesus. In short, it is a very radical business – which leads us to the second paving-stone on the way to hell: lack of love.

To understand this we must return to the parable with which we started this chapter – the frightening and challenging story of the sheep and the goats (Matt. 25:31–46). In that parable, Jesus pictures for us the Great Court of final judgment. The Judge (Jesus himself) announces the verdict. The sheep are to be received into heaven; the goats must depart to hell. The difference between them is simple and stark; it boils down to one single factor. In that story, it is certainly not a question of Christians (the sheep) to the right; and Buddhists, Marxists, Hindus, atheists, etc. (the goats) to the left.

No. At the Court of Judgment described in the parable, *both* groups claimed to follow Jesus; *both* groups addressed him as 'Lord'. *But only the first group understood what calling him Lord involves in practice.* They actively cared for the sick, the hungry, the lonely and the prisoners. The second group called Jesus 'Lord' with their lips, and left it at that.

In the New Testament, love has two opposites. The first is hatred; the second is indifference. In other words we are back with the argument developed in Chapters 8–12: the danger of shallow religion which is without challenge and without love.

At first sight it looks as if the sheep saved themselves by their acts of charity. But that is not the point of the story. Jesus himself holds the keys. He alone announces the verdict. He alone issues the invitation: 'Enter into the joy of your Lord.' We are not encouraged by this parable to return to a belief in the Score-card God, for as we have seen, that way leads to pride or despair.

No. The sheep are saved by God's grace; they enter heaven at the invitation of Jesus. Those men and women who are welcomed into heaven are sinners, like the rest of us. They find salvation because they prove by their deeds of love, that they really are his disciples. They call him Lord with their lips, *and* show that they mean it in their lives. Their attitude is summed up by St Paul in his letter to the Galatians, 'The only thing that counts is faith expressing itself through love' (Gal. 5:6).

In the face of such teaching we are challenged to reflect with some urgency upon the state of our own lives. To quote a terse comment often used by Jesus: 'He who has ears to hear, let him hear'. We are not all called to solve the problems of the economic injustice of the world – although some *are* called to get involved in these vital issues. We are not required to give that which we cannot give. Jesus insists instead that we 'think small'. A cup of cold water given to one child in need, or a visit made to one lonely person, is a very good day's work on his reckoning.

POSTSCRIPT

1   *A riddle*. Love is the only commodity which we can keep, only if we give it away. An old Sanskrit proverb puts it like this: you can only take with you in your two dead hands, what you have given away.

2   *The Last Supper*. Why does the account of the Last Supper in the Fourth Gospel not include the words of Jesus with which he instituted Holy Communion ('This is my body . . .'). We may see one reason in Chapter 6 – a 'sacramental chapter'. But perhaps there is another reason, too. Is it possible that by the time St John wrote, Christians were in danger of assuming that at the centre of their faith was an act of worship? So instead of including details of the Last Supper (already well-known), John included something else. Jesus, the Son of God, took a towel and washed

his disciples' feet. Love and humility must reign supreme – or we shall miss the true meaning of the Eucharist (which literally means 'thanksgiving'). In *Invitation to the New Testament* (DLT, 1967) Professor W. D. Davies wrote: 'To wash feet was fit only for slaves . . . To believe that Jesus took a towel, is to deliver human service from the deadly poison of triviality and to raise it to a divine status.'

3   *An important definition*. 'A real Christian is not only a good and well-intentioned person but a man or woman for whom Jesus Christ is ultimately decisive; for whom Jesus – not Caesar, not another god, not money, sex, power, or pleasure – is Lord'. Professor Hans Küng

Part 5

THE GLORY OF GOD

The world is charged with the grandeur of God.
Glory be to God for dappled things.
Gerard Manley Hopkins

Father of all, we give you thanks and praise,
that when we were still far off you met us in
Your Son and brought us home. Dying and living
He declared your love, gave us grace, and opened
the gate of glory . . .
ASB Holy Communion: Rite A

I implore you, good Jesus, that as in your mercy you have
given me to drink in with delight the words of your knowledge, so of your loving kindness you will also grant me one
day to come to you, the fountain of all wisdom, and to stand
forever before your face. Amen.
A prayer of the Venerable Bede.

O Lord, support us all the day long of this troublous life,
until the shades lengthen and the evening comes, and the
busy world is hushed, the fever of life is over and our work
done. Then, Lord, in thy mercy, grant us safe lodging, a
holy rest and peace at last; through Jesus Christ, our Lord.
Amen.
A prayer of Cardinal Newman.

20

GOD WHO OPENS WIDE THE GATES OF GLORY

We spent most of the previous chapter discussing the dour subject of hell, because the teaching of Jesus on this subject is too readily put on one side today. Few sermons are preached on the topic – even during the season of Advent which, at one time, always meant looking hard at the 'four last things': death, judgment, heaven and hell.

In this final chapter I am delighted to move from gloom to glory. Five questions in particular seem to haunt the modern mind on those rare occasions when we allow ourselves to consider unsavoury and frightening topics like death, judgment and eternity.

1 What is heaven like?

By its very nature we cannot know very fully – but we do find outline sketches in the New Testament. These suggest that modern worries about boredom ('sitting on a cloud twanging a harp all day') are without substance. Yes, there will be plenty of worship in heaven. But it will be worship with a difference. A multitude of voices raised in praise of Jesus, 'the Lamb upon the Throne', will make the finest earthly choir sound very ordinary – even massed voices singing Handel's Hallelujah Chorus!

But perhaps the most typical picture of heaven in the teaching of Jesus is that of a glorious party or banquet. Heaven will be marked by joy, by friendship, by celebration, by laughter and by festival.

2   Wishful thinking?

When I was a curate I visited an elderly woman who was very depressed. Her powers of speech had deteriorated, and she found communicating difficult and frustrating. One day she indicated that she wanted me to go to a particular drawer in her bedroom. I did so and found a photograph. The picture showed a strikingly beautiful young woman, and she got very excited. I thought the picture was of a favourite niece or grandchild. 'No, no, no.' So I questioned her, and at last I understood. The old woman in the bed, and the young woman in the photograph, were the same person: a mere sixty years separated the two.

Soon after that, she died. It is my firm belief that she is in heaven, and that she has been transformed into something – or rather someone – even more beautiful than she was in her teens. Just as the beauty of the tulip is related to the ugly bulb which is planted in the earth; just as the colourful butterfly arises from the inert chrysalis which it sheds and leaves behind – so will our life in heaven transcend our life on earth. Malcolm Muggeridge says that he is looking forward to death. He sees it as checking out of a second-rate hotel – and booking into something much more splendid.

Is such talk wishful thinking? Many people (some of them sorrowfully and wistfully) would say that it is. And they might go on to assert that evidence is out of the question. But the reality of heaven is as strong as the reality of the resurrection of Jesus. For if he really *did* rise from the dead, this has something very profound and important to say about life and death. For *our* resurrection is firmly linked to *his*.

Having studied it for many years, I am more than ever convinced that the evidence for the resurrection of Jesus from the dead is extremely strong. This is not the place to outline my reasons (see footnote on page 121) but we might note in passing that the evidence is strong enough to convince many people who are well-used to sifting data and drawing conclusions. The scholar-bishop, John Austin Baker, summed up the position when he wrote, 'It is still very important in a sceptical and often hostile culture, that the Easter story should stand up to attack – no easy matter at a distance of almost 2,000 years. But stand up it does' (*Evidence for the Resurrection*, Mowbray booklet, 1986).[1]

Belief in heaven is not wishful thinking if it is based on sound evidence. Of course the resurrection of Jesus is unique, but if it really happened, then it has enormous significance. For in the New Testament it is described as the 'first fruits' of a great harvest – which means that *his* resurrection from the dead stands as a guarantee of *our* resurrection, too.

Belief in heaven need not be escapism, either. It can be that of course. In some countries, at some points in history, the wealthy have encouraged the weak to endure terrible conditions by pointing them to 'pie in the sky when they die'. When this happens, religion really has become 'the opium of the people' (to use the phrase which appears to have been coined separately by the Christian Charles Kingsley and the Communist Karl Marx at about the same time).

It remains true that many influential reformers have been inspired by their belief in a personal heaven. They reasoned like this: if human beings really *are* made in the image of God; if they really *are* of eternal worth; if their ultimate home really *is* with God in heaven; then they deserve decent homes, full stomachs, hygienic drains and dignified care here on earth.

This was emphasised for me in J. G. Ballard's autobiographical novel *Empire of the Sun* (Gollancz, 1984). His book received fine reviews and was on the Booker prize short list. The film of the book was selected for the 1988 royal film performance. It tells the story of a boy who survived life in a Japanese prison camp. At one point, he describes the way in which he and two Christian missionaries were burying a dead comrade:

> The women pulled Mr Radik from the cart. Although wearied by the effort, they handled him with the same care they had shown when he was alive. Was he still alive

---

[1] Surprisingly – and significantly – the Jewish scholar Professor Pinchas Lapide also affirms his belief in the resurrection, in a recent book entitled *The Resurrection of Jesus* (Doubleday, 1985). Clearly he has no Christian axe to grind.

for these two Christian widows? Jim had always been impressed by strong religious beliefs. His mother and father were agnostics, and he respected devout Christians in the same way that he respected people who were members of the Graf Zeppelin Club or shopped at the Chinese department stores, for their mastery of an exotic foreign ritual. Besides, those who worked hardest for others, like Mrs Philips and Mrs Gilmour and Dr Ransome, often held beliefs that turned out to be correct.

3   What do we mean by 'the resurrection of the body'?

Those Christians who say the Apostles' Creed in Sunday worship, affirm their belief 'in the resurrection of the body'. What does this mean? I suppose my honest answer is – I'm not sure; but I believe it just the same! Now this reply sounds pretty unsatisfactory even to me, so I will hasten to enlarge on it.

In admitting my ignorance, I am underlining the fact that I don't pretend to have special insights into what happens beyond the grave. Like everyone else, I encounter problems which arise from using time and space language, to discuss issues which lie *beyond* time and space. Like everyone else I have the same limited (but sufficient) information which we find in the Bible. Which means that I am not operating primarily on the basis of speculation; I am operating mainly on the basis of *promises*.

Some people try to supplement these by other information, and growing interest has been shown in 'near-death experiences'. Many people who have nearly died, speak in similar terms about light, love, warmth, forgiveness and acceptance. Fascinating as these descriptions are, I doubt that they add much to our store of knowledge about life after death – although they often make a great and lasting impact on those involved. Others tread a more dangerous path . . .

I can understand what leads mourners into spiritualism. But I believe this activity to be profoundly misleading, and I would gently encourage those who are caught up in it, to talk with a minister from their local church. We must mourn and grieve for those who have died. And we are called to entrust them to the love of God. We are not required to attempt to 'bring them back' – indeed the Bible forbids us to do so.

Personality. The above is an important digression. But we must get back to our question. What is meant by 'the resurrection of the body'? There is no doubt that many people are much happier with the notion of a surviving 'spirit' or 'soul'. Some see this as adding our little drop of continuing consciousness to that of everyone else – and ultimately to that of God. If so, we continue to exist as a tiny drop in a great ocean of consciousness, but we lose our individuality. Others think of the human spirit waiting to be reborn in future children. (I recently heard this view stated by a regular church attender. He didn't actually use the word 'reincarnation' – a Hindu doctrine – but his views strongly implied this.)

The Bible is much more 'earthy'. It does talk of the human spirit surviving after death, but when it does so it usually speaks with dismay. 'Sheol' – the shadowy place of departed spirits often referred to in the Psalms – is to be feared because it is a twilight world without zest or vitality. When it talks of the glories of heaven, the Bible does so in terms of *physical resurrection*, rather than *spiritual survival*. By *resurrection* the New Testament writers do not mean mere *resuscitation*. What is raised will be far more glorious than what is 'sown' – just as the butterfly is much lovelier than the chrysalis.

Modern minds addressing this difficult – but fascinating and important – subject sometimes find it helpful to focus on the word 'personality'. The teaching of the Bible is that we shall retain our personalities – refined and purified – for all eternity. You will still be recognisably *you*. We shall be much more interesting and glorious than we are now, but there will be a definite link between you-as-you-are-now, and you-as-you-will-be-then.

Every aspect of your life and personality which you offered to God during your earthly life, will be gloriously raised – and handed back to you. In heaven, we shall not lose our identity in an ocean of consciousness. Indeed, it is only *then* that we shall really find and possess our true identity. For the gifts which make us what we are, are *on loan* now. They will be *given* to us then – and they will be ours for ever.

This stress on personality removes crude (but, for some, pressing) questions concerning loved ones who have been buried or cremated. How can they be raised? Mercifully, resurrection does not depend upon God reassembling our human frame. After all, by the renewal of the cells which make up our bodies, we each get a new body every seven years, even in *this* life!

In closing this short section – an illustration. I recall visiting someone who was very ill. He had no colour in his cheeks, and little energy. From time to time a little of his 'real self' peeped through, as he made a joke at his own expense, and gave a wry smile. Some months later I met him again, after he had recovered from his illness. He was the same person all right – but he was quite different, too! Full of energy and vitality. That experience provides a hint of the way in which, by God's power and love, we shall be changed.

The New Testament phrase 'eternal life' refers to a quality of life as well as to life everlasting. It begins, not when we die, but when we first turn to Christ as Lord and Liberator. But the quality of our life in heaven will far surpass its present standard – just as my friend's level of vitality was quite different during and after his illness.

4 How do we get to heaven?

The New Testament answer is clear enough. Absolutely no one is good enough for heaven. '. . . for all have sinned and fall short of the glory of God' (Rom. 3:23). We can only find salvation by the grace and mercy of a living, loving God.

The ancient Church of the Nativity in Bethlehem's Manger Square is a large building with a small and low doorway. By this means, every visitor is reminded that we can enter the presence of the infant King only by bending low: for we must approach in lowliness and humility. These same qualities are required for entry into his presence in heaven too.

5 Can we be sure of getting there?

On this question the New Testament speaks with two voices. Yes, we can and should be confident. 'Therefore, there is now no condemnation for those who are in Christ Jesus' (Rom. 8:1). Because *he* has defeated sin and death, and opened wide the gate of glory, *we* can go in. However, there is another strong strand running through the New Testament as well. We should not be *overconfident*. Examine yourself. Remember the parable of the sheep and the goats and ask: when I call Jesus 'Lord', do I really mean it? And do I show it by visiting the sick, welcoming the stranger, and giving to those in need?

I have known people get hopping mad on hearing Christians speak with confidence about the fact that they will go to heaven when they die. It seems so arrogant. They appear to be too sure of themselves. But this criticism misses the point. Salvation means rescue. It depends not upon our own efforts and goodness, but upon the efforts and goodness of Jesus. The safety of a man in a rubber dinghy in the middle of the ocean, depends entirely upon the navigation skills of the helicopter pilot. Once he has thrown up his last flare, the lost man can do nothing but entrust himself to the rescue services. The children's hymn puts this rather more theologically,

There was no other good enough to pay the price of sin;
He only could unlock the gate of heaven, and let us in.

Jesus has assured us that in his house there are many mansions. It would be arrogant not to believe him.

In closing, a story might illustrate the point. I was invited to visit a friend who told me that there would be someone at home to meet me. In case I was late (and it was a long journey) I was told to let myself in – the key would be under a plant-pot in the garden shed. Now my friend is not very well organised, and as I sat in a traffic jam I was unsure that I would manage to get in on arrival. My fears were well founded. When I arrived, there was no one at home and no key to be found. I walked round the house, but I was not good enough at climbing drain-pipes to break in.

The following summer my friend got married, and the

invitation was renewed. This time his wife wrote to me. She assured me that she would be in between 4 and 6 p.m., and she enclosed a key in case I was delayed.

On this occasion I set out on my journey with great confidence. For my entry into the house did not depend upon my own promptness, nor upon the word of someone I only half-trusted. My confidence was based upon the promise of someone I knew to be reliable. In any case I had been given a key. Two good reasons for confidence, neither of which added up to *self*-confidence. For everything depended on *her*. My part was pretty small – I had only to accept her word, and to use the key which she had provided.

> Death, be not proud, though some have called thee
> Mighty and dreadful, for thou art not so . . .
> One short sleep past, we wake eternally,
> And death shall be no more. Death, thou shalt die.
>   John Donne

PRACTICAL POSTSCRIPT: WHERE NOW?

At the beginning of this book, I emphasised that faith in God is a dynamic concept. It isn't an 'interesting idea'. Properly understood, it connects with real life. So at the end of our journey, I encourage you to take a few leisurely minutes to do some personal stocktaking. As a starting-point, I suggest that we consider the lovely phrase with which we end some Holy Communion Services.

> Go in peace to love and serve the Lord,
> In the name of Christ. Amen.

1 *Go in peace*. Not: go into a peaceful world. But: go in peace. For the world into which we go is often turbulent, troubled and divided. If we are to go in peace, we must take our peace with us – for we shall not find it in the world. That peace – which passes all understanding – is a gift from God.

If you want God's peace, quietly ask for it now.

2 *Serve the Lord*. God's peace is not for you alone; it is to be received and shared. You may feel unworthy; you may be afraid. No matter: it has never been any different. God has always used people like you and me – inadequate people who are willing to be used.

Some 750 years before Jesus, the prophet Isaiah caught a glimpse of the holiness and majesty of God. God in his greatness; God in his otherness; God in his burning purity. Isaiah was overcome with a deep sense of unworthiness: '"Woe to me!" I cried. "I am ruined! For I am a man of unclean lips . . . and my eyes have seen the King, the Lord Almighty"' (Isa. 6:5).

But the holy Lord is the merciful Lord. He assured Isaiah of forgiveness, and he asked: 'Who will go for us?' Isaiah did not hesitate: 'Here am I. Send me!' (Isa. 6:8).

If you want to serve God, then, like Isaiah, you must receive forgiveness first. So, in quietness and stillness, ask God to forgive you. Then, to prove (to yourself) that you mean business, perform some definite act of service – the first of many. Visit a lonely person, or write a neglected letter, or offer an overdue apology, or . . .

3 *Love the Lord*. Jesus taught us to *fear* God, to *trust* God, and to *love* God. Love warms up the whole process. Service can be grim duty, but love is warm and personal. At its centre, Christianity is not a code of ethics; it is not even a way of life. At root it is a loving relationship with the living

God, through the risen Christ, in the power of the Holy Spirit.

We show our love for God by loving other people (who are also made in the image of God); by caring for his creation; and by spending time in his presence – in worship, prayer and Bible study.

If you want to love God, ask him to pour his love into your heart.

Heavenly Father, true and living God, we ask you to give us your peace, to inspire us with your love, and to give us perseverance in your service. Amen.

A Final Challenge from Archbishop Desmond Tutu

Students sometimes don't know the answers to exam questions and they produce those gems called howlers. Once in a scripture exam the students were asked, 'What did John the Baptist say to Jesus when He came to be baptized?' Well this chap (I don't think it was a chappess) did not know the answer, but was going to have a shot at it, and wrote, 'John the Baptist said to Jesus, "Remember you are the Son of God and behave like one!"'

Well, remember you are princes and princesses, God's loved ones – behave like one

'Grace and peace to you from God our Father and the Lord Jesus Christ' (Phil. 1:2).